Strategies for Successful Student Teaching

Related Titles of Interest

Current Issues and Trends in Education
Jerry Aldridge & Renitta Goldman
ISBN: 0-321-07978-7

**Impact Teaching: Ideas and Strategies
for Teachers to Maximize Student
Learning**
Richard Howell Allen
ISBN: 0-205-33414-8

**The Way Schools Work: A Sociological Analysis
of Education, Third Edition**
Kathleen Bennett de Marrais & Margaret LeCompte
ISBN: 0-8013-1956-0

**New Teacher's Performance-Based Guide to
Culturally Diverse Classrooms**
Timothy R. Blair
ISBN: 0-205-38206-1

**How to Develop a Professional Portfolio:
A Manual for Teachers, Third Edition**
Dorothy M. Campbell, Pamela Bondi Cignetti,
Beverly J. Melenyzer, Diane H. Nettles,
& Richard M. Wyman
ISBN: 0-205-39341-1

**Researching Teaching: Exploring Teacher
Development Through Reflexive Inquiry**
Ardra L. Cole & J. Gary Knowles
ISBN: 0-205-18076-0

**Developing a Professional Teaching Portfolio:
A Guide for Educators**
Patricia Costantino & Marie De Lorenzo
ISBN: 0-205-32955-1

**The Moral Stake in Education: Contested
Premises and Practices**
Joan F. Goodman & Howard Lesnick
ISBN: 0-321-02340-4

**The Digital Teaching Portfolio Handbook:
A How-To Guide for Educators**
Clare R. Kilbane & Natalie B. Milman
ISBN: 0-205-34345-7

**Your First Year of Teaching and Beyond,
Fourth Edition**
Ellen L. Kronowitz
ISBN: 0-205-38156-1

**Life in Schools: An Introduction to Critical
Pedagogy in the Foundations of Education,
Fourth Edition**
Peter McLaren
ISBN: 0-205-35118-2

Handbook for the Beginning Teacher
Courtney W. Moffatt & Thomas L. Moffatt
ISBN: 0-205-34372-4

How to Get a Teaching Job
Courtney W. Moffatt & Thomas L. Moffatt
ISBN: 0-205-29924-5

**Teaching and Schooling in America: Pre- and
Post-September 11**
Allan Ornstein
ISBN: 0-205-36711-9

**Ask the Teacher: A Practitioner's Guide to
Teaching and Learning in the Diverse
Classroom**
Mark Ryan
ISBN: 0-205-37076-4

**Teaching Convictions: Critical Ethical Issues
and Education**
Patrick Slattery & Dana Rapp
ISBN: 0-321-05401-6

**Teaching to the Standards of Effective Practice:
A Guide to Becoming a Successful Teacher**
Robert Wandberg & John Rohwer
ISBN: 0-205-34407-0

For further information on these and other related
titles, contact:
  College Division
  ALLYN AND BACON, INC.
  75 Arlington Street, Suite 300
  Boston, MA 02116
  www.ablongman.com

STRATEGIES FOR SUCCESSFUL STUDENT TEACHING

A Comprehensive Guide

Second Edition

Carol Marra Pelletier
Boston College

Boston   New York   San Francisco
Mexico City   Montreal   Toronto   London   Madrid   Munich   Paris
Hong Kong   Singapore   Tokyo   Cape Town   Sydney

This handbook is dedicated to CDL

Executive Editor and Publisher: Stephen D. Dragin
Senior Editorial Assistant: Barbara Strickland
Manufacturing Buyer: Andrew Turso
Marketing Manager: Tara Whorf
Cover Designer: Suzanne Harbison
Production Coordinator: Pat Torelli Publishing Services
Editorial-Production Service: TKM Productions
Electronic Composition: TKM Productions

For related titles and support materials, visit our online catalog at www.ablongman.com.

Library of Congress Cataloging-in-Publication Data

Pelletier, Carol Marra.
    Strategies for successful student teaching : a comprehensive guide / Carol Marra
Pelletier.-- 2nd ed.
        p. cm.
    ISBN 0-205-39682-8
        1. Student teaching--United States--Handbooks, manuals, etc. 2. Student
    teachers--Training of--United States--Handbooks, manuals, etc. I. Title.

    LB2157.U5P392003
    370'.71-dc21

                                    2003043797

Contents

Chapter 7   Instructional Strategies for Diverse Learners: How Do I Teach to Varied Student Needs?   155

Foreword

Strategies for Successful Student Teaching is an excellent, practical guide for student teachers. It gives them a road map of what to expect and the steps to take for a successful journey into the teaching profession. Not only does it introduce teachers to an array of strategies for having a successful student teaching experience but it also creates a powerful vision of teaching and learning.

Learning to teach is complex. Student teaching offers prospective teachers an opportunity to learn alongside exemplary experienced teachers. It provides an opportunity to integrate theory and practice in a classroom context, working daily with students. But what contributes to a successful experience, and how can we design programs that support the development of the next generation of outstanding teachers?

Having supervised hundreds of student teachers at the University of California, Santa Cruz, I believe that quality preservice programs are grounded in components of professional development such as collaboration, collegiality, and community among teachers. This book offers student teachers, cooperating teachers, and teacher supervisors opportunities to interact with one another as they negotiate and better understand the practical activity of teaching in a classroom setting.

Student teachers are encouraged to build their own community to share what they learn and to reflect together on what makes for excellence in teaching. The kinds of questions that are posed throughout the text encourage interaction and joint problem solving. Student teachers learn to constantly assess and revise their teaching practices. This approach builds

teachers' self-confidence and lays the groundwork for the kind of collaborative approach to teacher professional development that distinguishes successful schools.

The creation of a teaching portfolio is central to the process of reflection and assessment and one that Dr. Pelletier focuses on specifically. The portfolio process offers preservice teachers a means of documenting their growth throughout their student teaching. It demonstrates the relationship between teaching, learning, and assessment, and encourages critical examination of classroom practice.

The challenge facing those responsible for the education of the next generation of teachers is to provide equitable and effective schooling for all students. This book helps teachers grapple with theories that have special relevance to the education and schooling of culturally diverse students.

As students work through the three sections of the book, "Preparing for the Practicum Experience," "Classroom Practice during Student Teaching," and "Completing the Practicum Experience," they are introduced not only to excellent pedagogy but also to a vision of what it means to be a teacher dedicated to lifelong learning and to advancing the achievement of all children. Pelletier has done an outstanding job of providing a student teacher handbook that is as inspirational as it is practical.

Ellen Moir
Executive Director
New Teacher Center at the
University of California, Santa Cruz

Preface

This handbook serves as a comprehensive guide for you as you begin your full-time student teaching. It starts with the question, "Why do I want to be a teacher?" and moves through to the creation of a portfolio, the job search, and a checklist for accepting your first teaching position. To my knowledge, no such book exists at this time that begins with the first steps of student teaching and follows through to the first teaching position.

Strategies for Successful Student Teaching is not a substitute for teacher education courses, methods, or strategies provided for preservice student teachers at the university. It is designed to support these courses and serves as a reminder of what you have completed as part of your formal preparation to become teachers. As student teachers, you are not expected to complete all the activities, but rather to select the ones that relate to your level and experience. As comprehensive as this handbook is, there are probably activities that are not included here that you may find you need. Create them with the assistance of your cooperating teacher and university supervisor to ensure that you have a complete experience.

As you begin your student teaching, you will be excited, nervous, and full of questions. I hope this handbook answers your questions and takes some of the nervousness away as it guides you through a successful student teaching experience. Good Luck!

ACKNOWLEDGMENTS

This book is the result of many years of observing student teachers, reflecting on practice, listening to cooperating teachers, and collaborating with the clinical faculty supervisors at Boston College. It is a synthesis of hundreds of conversations, thoughts, ideas, and readings.

I am grateful to Kathy O'Connor and Betty Davidson for their support and encouragement. They offered many suggestions to this second edition, resulting in more examples included for secondary student teachers. I also thank the following reviewers for their comments: Paul B. Cooley (Gonzaga University), Linda M. Holdman (University of North Dakota), Paul H. Matthews (University of Georgia), and Iran Pelcyger (Bronx Community College of the City University of New York).

Special thanks to the Boston College student teachers who continue to share their needs, questions, and ideas with me. They are the inspiration for this work.

Chapter 1

Teaching as a Professional Career Choice

Preparing for Student Teaching: Am I Ready?

Begin now to prepare yourself! Do not run out and buy a teacher's plan book or a new pack of pencils for your future students. Instead, take some time to think about what you are about to do and the path you are on as you move from a pre-service teacher to an in-service teacher. You are a lot farther than you think. Don't blink; it will be over before you even know it.

Student Teacher

Why did you decide to become a teacher? Did you always want to teach? Did you have an inspiring teacher during your years in school? Did you have teachers you didn't like and want to create a different experience than you had in school? The reason is important for you to think about as you begin to prepare for your student teaching experience. Revisit your commitment and choice to this profession. Is this your first career or are you changing careers after trying something else? All these questions are important as you reflect on the events in your life that have led you to student teaching.

Teaching is more than a job. It is a way of life for those who choose it. Some even say it is a "calling" for special people. Others may not feel the same way about teachers and the profession, and that is why teachers are often underpaid, overworked, undervalued, and criticized by the public, parents, and their own students. So why would anyone want to be a teacher?

Many teachers say it has been the small things that have kept them in teaching: the smile on a student's face when he finally understands a concept, observing a student reading a book for the first time, or challenging a student to strive for higher goals. There is also a built-in sense of renewal each year when one class leaves and moves on and a new group enters the classroom. Teachers have shared that although it is often sad to let the students go, there is excitement in being able to challenge a new group.

Intrinsic rewards are not enough for many teachers today, as is evidenced in their choice to leave the classroom after a few years because the realities of everyday life in the day-to-day context of the profession are difficult. Why didn't they understand this during their preparation? Everyone says teaching is hard, yet student teachers' idealism often outweighs the challenge and possibility of failure.

Preparing for student teaching is as important as participating in your semester or year-long experience. Take the time to inventory how well prepared you are for entering the classroom, to think about your commitment to the profession, and to determine your personal reasons for becoming a teacher.

As a student teacher, you need to think about the following areas of preparation: (1) academic subject, (2) early field experiences, (3) teaching strategies and methods, (4) emotional readiness, and (5) commitment to the profession. Are you prepared in all these ways?

The activities and ideas in this chapter will assist you in surveying who you are as a beginning teacher and allow you to see where any "gaps" in your preparation may be so that you can address them during student teaching. Remember the purpose of the experience is to allow you to "experience" the rigors and joys of a classroom. Make student teaching the top priority in your life right now. Put all your energy into your teaching, learn as much as you can, experience the school, work with your cooperating teacher, and enjoy the learning curve you will be on.

DEFINITION OF TERMS

This handbook will use the following terms interchangeably:

student teaching — practicum experience — clinical experience — field experience
A five-day-a-week, full-time experience in a school for the purpose of completing requirements for certification to become a teacher

clinical faculty — university supervisor — college supervisor
The person from the teacher preparation program who visits the student teacher and observes lessons

cooperating teacher — cooperating practitioner
The teacher at the school site who hosts the student teacher in her or his classroom

Field Office — Office of Practicum Experiences — Field Placement Office — Field Experiences
The office that coordinates all field placements, supervision, and certification

Career Center — Career Planning and Placement Office — Career Services
The office on campus that assists students in finding teaching positions

GUIDING PRINCIPLES

A new section titled, *Discussing Professional Standards* is included in this second edition of *Strategies for Successful Student Teaching.* The Interstate New Teacher Assessment & Support Consortium (INTASC) principles serve as a focus for discussions with your supervisor and cooperating teacher, as well as a reminder that National Professional Standards guide the teaching profession.

Each chapter will introduce one or more principles and also suggest that you review them throughout the practicum. The principles are easy to read and make perfect sense—what is difficult is seeing how they actually apply to your work with students. What do they really mean? How will they look in your classroom? What observable behaviors will you demonstrate that relate to these principles? These are more complicated questions. The social context of your classroom and school will impact the ways in which you apply these principles.

Abbreviated Version of the INTASC
Principles (detailed description in ACT Process 1.6)

The teacher ...

#1   understands the discipline and can make subject matter meaningful

#2   understands how children learn and can provide support

#3   understands and provides opportunities for diverse learners

#4   understands and uses a variety of instructional strategies

#5   uses an understanding of behavior to create a positive environment

#6   uses knowledge of communication to foster collaboration and support

#7   plans instruction based on subject, students, community, curriculum

#8   understands and uses formal and informal assessment

#9   is a reflective practitioner who seeks opportunities to grow

#10   fosters relationships with colleagues, parents, and agencies to support students

Chapter	Principles Introduced	Principles Reviewed
1 Career	1 and 9	
2 Getting Started	10	9
3 Supervision		9 and 10
4 Classroom Management	2 and 5	
5 Behavior Management	6	2 and 5
6 Planning	7	1 and 2
7 Strategies	3 and 4	2 and 7
8 Assessment	8	10
9 Completing		All
10 Job Portfolio		All
11 Job Search		All
12 The First Year		All

HOW THIS GUIDE IS ORGANIZED

This comprehensive guide is organized into three major parts:

- **Part I   Preparing for the Practicum Experience**
  Chapters 1 through 3 provide an overview to the guide as well as specific strategies for starting the practicum off successfully. The text also includes what you can expect from the supervision process.

- **Part II   Classroom Practice during Student Teaching**
  Chapters 4 through 8 provide an overview of the main ideas and topics that guide classroom practice and promote student learning.

- **Part III   Completing the Practicum Experience**
  Chapters 9 through 12 provide specific ideas and suggestions for culminating the experience as well as strategies for the interview portfolio and the job search. The last chapter guides you to your first year in your own classroom.

Each chapter begins with a short narrative that serves as an overview to the chapter topic. Following that narrative you will find a page is dedicated to **Discussing Professional Standards** through *Quality Conversations* with your cooperating teacher. The goal of this activity is to focus your thinking on current Interstate New Teacher Assessment & Support Consortium (INTASC) principles and how they relate to your student teaching.

Furthermore, the chapters are organized around the topics of **PLAN, CONNECT, ACT**, and **REFLECT**. Each topic offers questions, samples, and ideas to think about. This "hands-on" guide is designed to be written in or copied and used for multiple uses.

The **PLAN** pages include *Use Advice from Former Student Teachers, Key Questions* for the chapter, suggestions for how to *Take Care of Yourself and Avoid Stress* during student teaching, as well as a format for how to *Plan Your Week*.

The **CONNECT** pages outline People, Readings & Resources, and Technology websites that will assist you in bringing the most current information to your practice.

The **ACT** pages of the chapter include a variety of processes to be completed alone or with your cooperating teacher, your university supervisor, or other student teachers. These *processes* are designed to stimulate your thinking as you progress through your practicum. They are useful for student teachers at all levels and can be easily adapted for discussions as well as for individual written reflection.

The **REFLECT** pages include stems that will guide your *Inquiry* into daily practice, *Self-Reflection,* and ways to review the *Critiques* offered to you by your cooperating teacher and university supervisor.

SUGGESTED WAYS TO USE THIS BOOK

The book is designed for full practicum student teachers in five-day-a-week field assignments who are completing a semester-long 14- to 16-week experience. It can be easily adapted for shorter experiences or expanded for year-long student teaching experiences. Chapters on observation, lesson planning, and instruction are also appropriate for prepracticum experiences with student teachers who may be taking a methods course and completing a one- or two-day field experience.

There are benefits and value to all who are involved with the student teaching experience. First, you clearly benefit from this opportunity as you are welcomed into an experienced teacher's classroom. The opportunity to try the methods you have learned and talked about through your teacher preparation program is finally here. To observe and be part of a school community prior to entering the profession as an employee is a unique opportunity. Through your own CONNECTions and REFLECTions, you will learn about yourself as a teacher—what you feel comfortable with and what you still need to learn. Teaching is a profession of lifelong learning. Remember that as a teacher you will always be a learner, too.

The university supervisor and practicum office that placed you in your student teaching assignment benefits from and values the relationships with the schools and teachers who have said yes to a student teacher. These individuals listen and learn from the schools and shape the university programs to meet both your needs and the needs of the schools. They learn from student teachers as well through critical conversations about the key questions and by developing models of supervision that promote inquiry. Supervisors remain critical friends to the experience, and their goal is to bring a quality teacher to the profession.

Suggested Reading Schedule

Chapter	Title	When to Read	When to Use
Chapter 1	Teaching as a Professional Career Choice	Prior to practicum	Beginning
Chapter 2	Getting Started at the School	Prior to practicum	Beginning
Chapter 3	Supervision during Student Teaching	Week 1	Entire practicum
Chapter 4	Classroom Management: Organizing Time and Space for Effective Teaching and Learning	Week 2	Entire practicum
Chapter 5	Behavior Management and Discipline Strategies	Weeks 2–3	Entire practicum
Chapter 6	Daily Lesson and Unit Planning	Weeks 2–3	Entire practicum
Chapter 7	Instructional Strategies for Diverse Learners	Weeks 4–6	Entire practicum
Chapter 8	Assessing, Documenting, and Communicating Student Progress	Weeks 6–9	Entire practicum
Chapter 9	Completing the Practicum Experience	Two weeks before final date of completion	Culmination
Chapter 10	Designing an Interview Portfolio	Final Weeks	For job interview
Chapter 11	The Search for a Teaching Position	Final Weeks	For first position
Chapter 12	Lifelong Learning for a Career in Teaching	Final Weeks	For success as a teacher

The cooperating schools also benefit from having you in their classrooms and schools. Many teachers have commented that they love the energy and new ideas. They want to welcome you into their world not only to share what they have learned through their experiences but also to learn from you. These teachers are key to your success as a student teacher. Student teachers are more than an extra set of hands—they are enthusiastic, contributing members of a team. Are you valued by the schools? Ask any cooperating teacher who has had a successful experience and he or she will answer with an enthusiastic YES! The value of student teachers has also been expressed in the many job offers made to students as they near completion of their program.

Finally, the value to the students you work with is immeasurable. Students love student teachers. They relate to them and often receive much attention in a large classroom. You make a difference to those students. Do you remember any student teachers in your classrooms? What did you feel the benefits were?

This book is written with the spirit of *success* and *retention* in mind—*success* for the student teaching experience to be a wonderful experience of growth and new learning, and *retention* in that you will choose to stay in the teaching profession and commit to it as your career choice.

Discussing Professional Standards

QUALITY CONVERSATIONS TO ENHANCE STUDENT LEARNING

National standards guide new teacher preparation in the United States. The INTASC created 10 principles for effective teaching. These principles are offered to you as a way to focus your attention on these key elements of practice. The "bottom line" is all about student learning. Are your students learning? How do you know?

Use these pages in each chapter to frame a quality conversation with your cooperating teacher and university supervisor. Don't be afraid to ask your own questions, too. Also use the REFLECT pages at the end of each chapter to deepen your thinking and to continue your quality conversations throughout the practium experience and into your first year of teaching.

INTASC Principles

Focus for Chapter 1

Principle #1 The teacher understands the central concepts, tools of inquiry, and structures of the discipline(s) he or she teaches and can create learning experiences that make these aspects of subject matter meaningful for students.

Principle #9 The teacher is a reflective practitioner who continually evaluates the effects of his or her choices and actions of others (students, parents, and other professionals in the learning community) and who actively seeks out opportunities to grow professionally.

ASK YOURSELF What do these principles mean to me right now? How will I know if I have achieved these principles?

DISCUSS WITH YOUR SUPERVISOR OR COOPERATING TEACHER

How will your supervisor/cooperating teacher know if you have achieved these principles? What evidence will you have to demonstrate these skills to them?

How will you know if your students have learned as a result of your teaching?

PLAN

USE ADVICE FROM FORMER STUDENT TEACHERS

Talk to student teachers who have just completed the experience and review the tips below to guide you.

- Take some time to think about *why* you want to become a teacher. Use the process in this chapter to guide you. Share your thoughts with your supervisor.
- Get Organized NOW! Crates, notebooks, files, and boxes will help.
- Free up your schedule so you can fully immerse yourself in student teaching. You don't want to have to leave school early to run to another commitment.

PROCESS YOUR EXPERIENCE

Respond to the Key Questions below by completing the process pages in each chapter. These ACTs will encourage you to deepen your thinking about teaching and learning. Write on the pages and save them to review at the end of the experience.

KEY QUESTIONS

1. Why did I choose teaching?

2. How prepared am I to begin my student teaching?

3. What is missing and how can I integrate it into my student teaching?

4. What will be expected of me for successful completion of the practicum?

5. What are my goals and expectations for student teaching?

PLAN

TAKE CARE OF YOURSELF AND AVOID STRESS

Plan to avoid the typical stresses of student teaching by following advice from cooperating teachers and university supervisors.

EXERCISE!

Design a plan for yourself so you can get regular exercise and sleep during your student teaching experience. This is not the time to stop taking care of yourself. Now, more than ever, you will need activities to balance your active day of thinking and teaching.

What can you do? Before school? At lunch time? After school? Run, yoga, jog, join a gym, bike, read, walk, or meditate.

What will *you* do to prevent stress?

PLAN YOUR WEEK

Priority List

Done	Tasks	Priority	Complete by When?

Place things to do on the day you would like to do them.

Monday Date:	Tuesday Date:	Wednesday Date:	Thursday Date:	Friday Date:

CONNECT

CONNECT is a resource page with ideas and suggestions to support you during student teaching. Select and complete any CONNECT items that will enhance your experience in the classroom.

CONNECT with people

- Your college practicum office
  Have you applied to be supervised in addition to registering for the field courses required?
- Favorite teachers, parents, guardians, or significant adults in your life
  How have they influenced you? Are they teachers?
- Student teachers
  Talk to some friends who have just finished student teaching. Ask what they learned about themselves as beginning teachers and ask for any advice they have to offer you.

CONNECT with readings & resources

- College handbook, practicum handbook, and syllabus requirements
  Review mission, policies, procedures, requirements, and deadlines.
- Books and authors to explore on the Internet or at your local library
  Becoming a Teacher: A Practical and Political School Survival Guide by Grusko and Krame (Grayson Bernard)
  Enhancing Professional Practice by Danielson (ASCD)
  The Complex World of Teaching edited by Mintz and Yun (Harvard)
  Improving Schools From Within by Barth (Jossey-Bass)
  Courage to Teach by Palmer (Jossey-Bass)
  Teaching: Making Sense of an Uncertain Craft by McDonald (Teachers College)

CONNECT technology to teaching

- Read *World Wide Web for Teachers* by Cafolla et al. (Allyn and Bacon)
- Explore and discover websites. Try these:
  Teaching in Elementary/Secondary School = http://www.ericsp.org
  Education Week = http://www.edweek.org
  Become familiar with educational issues = http://www.familyedge.com
  For first-year teachers = http://www.datasync.com/~teachers/

ACT
Process 1.1 Why Did I Choose Teaching?
Documenting My Journey

PAST

1. Describe your first memories of thinking about becoming a teacher.

2. List any names of people who affected your decision to become a teacher.

3. Who were some of your favorite teachers and why do you still remember them?

PRESENT

4. How do you feel right now about beginning your student teaching and becoming a teacher? On a separate sheet of paper draw a picture of how you see yourself teaching in a classroom.

Note: At the end of your experience, you will draw another picture of yourself in the classroom and have an opportunity to compare your drawings.

FUTURE

5. Where do you see yourself in five years?

Share these thoughts and your drawing with your supervisor or cooperating teacher and use them as a focus for a journal entry.

ACT
Process 1.2 How Ready Am I?
Creating a Student Teacher Profile

Complete and share with your university supervisor.

Name: _____ **College/University:** _____

Address: _____ **Phone:** _____ **E-mail:** _____

_____ **Major:** _____

Field of Certification: _____ **Grade Level:** _____

1. Attach your college transcript or a list of courses completed prior to student teaching to document your knowledge base in the subject(s) you will be teaching.

2. List any courses you have taken that relate to child development, adolescent psychology, and similar subjects.

   _____

   _____

3. List any pre-practicum experiences or other teaching experiences.

Date of Pre-practicum	**School**	**Grade Level**

4. List your skills, hobbies, areas of expertise or interest (e.g., foreign language or travel, musical ability, drama, dance, sports, coaching).

   _____

   _____

5. Highlight all teaching methods courses on your transcript.

6. Are you feeling emotionally ready and confident to teach this semester?

   _____

7. What is your commitment to the teaching profession?

   _____

   _____

Review this inventory sheet and decide with your supervisor where you may anticipate needing support.

ACT
Process 1.3 Linking Theory and Practice
Using Prior Knowledge

Collect and organize all the resources and ideas you have completed in your preparation to become a teacher. List the ideas here and then find your materials and organize them for easy access later.

1. List any lesson plans from pre-practicum experiences that may be useful in full practicum.

   _____

   _____

   _____

2. List any books you would like to use this semester.

   _____

   _____

   _____

3. List any kits, manipulatives, documents, displays, or resources you would like to incorporate into your teaching this semester/year.

   _____

   _____

   _____

4. List any teacher idea books, magazines, journals, or other information that would be helpful.

   _____

   _____

   _____

ACT
Process 1.4 My Goals and Expectations
for the Practicum Experience
What Do I Expect from My Student Teaching?

1. What are my learning goals? Sample goals could be

    to learn how to manage a classroom effectively

    to take risks in using technology in the classroom

    to teach a history lesson that engages and excites all the students

    My personal goals are

    to _____

    to _____

    to _____

2. What do I expect of my cooperating teacher?

    _____

    _____

    _____

3. What does my cooperating teacher expect from me and why did he or she agree to accept a student teacher?

    _____

    _____

    _____

4. What do I expect from my college supervisor?

    _____

    _____

    _____

Your supervisor will share college expectations at your first three-way meeting if you do not have a syllabus before that time.

Communicate your goals and expectations to these key people to clarify everyone's perceptions and expectations for the experience. Avoid misunderstanding and unfulfilled expectations!

ACT
Process 1.5 What Do I Need to Know about Professional Standards?
Guidelines for the Profession

Multiple frameworks are currently used for organizing and assessing teacher competency. Review the national, state, and college guidelines for your teacher preparation program and ask questions if you do not understand the standards by which the public measures teacher competency. Use the Internet to read about each professional group's mission and criteria.

NATIONAL GUIDELINES

☐ NBPTS (National Board for Professional Teaching Standards)—Offers teachers the equivalent of an advanced degree in medicine. This is voluntary.

☐ INTASC (Interstate New Teacher Assessment & Support Consortium)—Proposes standards primarily for new teachers and is compatible with NBPTS.

☐ NASDTEC (National Association of State Directors of Teacher Education and Certification)—Provides standards for teachers.

☐ NCATE (National Council of Accreditation of Teacher Education)—Provides standards for teacher education college programs to use as a guide for creating quality programs.

☐ Praxis Series (replacing the National Teacher Examination, NTE)—Praxis III includes a performance assessment component with criteria for classroom teaching called Pathwise, which some colleges are using as a basis of performance in field experiences.

☐ Professional organizations in all subject areas also have their own criteria and performance expectations for teachers. Check your educational resource library for the most current websites for the national teachers professional organizations that relate to your field.

☐ Other _____

Which national guidelines govern your teacher preparation program?

STATE GUIDELINES

The state competencies will be an integral component of your student teaching program. Become familiar with them and be sure you understand how each competency translates into an observable behavior in the field.

☐ Certification Competencies—Review and list your state competencies.

☐ Curriculum Frameworks—Does your state have guidelines for curriculum that you should be familiar with before you enter the classroom? Use the Internet to find out and ask your director of practicum experiences how you can learn about state initiatives.

☐ Principles of Effective Teaching—Are teachers assessed in a consistent way statewide? If your state has a state evaluation instrument for in-service teachers, you can review it by asking the teachers in your district when you begin student teaching. This gives you a context for understanding how in-service teachers are assessed.

☐ Other _____

This guide will use these principles as a framework for looking at teaching and learning. Use *Quality Conversations to Enhance Student Learning* on the *Discussing Professional Standards* pages at the beginning of each chapter to analyze each principle with your cooperating teacher or supervisor.

Principle #1 The teacher understands the central concepts, tools of inquiry, and structures of the discipline(s) he or she teaches and can create learning experiences that make these aspects of subject matter meaningful for students.

Principle #2 The teacher understands how children learn and develop, and can provide learning opportunities that support their intellectual, social, and personal development.

Principle #3 The teacher understands how students differ in their approaches to learning and creates instructional opportunities that are adapted to diverse learners.

Principle #4 The teacher understands and uses a variety of instructional strategies to encourage students' development of critical thinking, problem solving, and performance skills.

Principle #5 The teacher uses an understanding of individual and group motivation and behavior to create a learning environment that encourages positive social interaction, active engagement in learning, and self-motivation.

Principle #6 The teacher uses knowledge of effective verbal, nonverbal, and media communication techniques to foster active inquiry, collaboration, and supportive interaction in the classroom.

Principle #7 The teacher plans instruction based on knowledge of subject matter, students, the community, and curriculum goals.

Principle #8 The teacher understands and uses formal and informal assessment strategies to evaluate and ensure the continuous intellectual, social, and physical development of the learner.

Principle #9 The teacher is a reflective practitioner who continually evaluates the effects of his or her choices and actions of others (students, parents, and other professionals in the learning community) and who actively seeks out opportunities to grow professionally.

Principle #10 The teacher fosters relationships with school colleagues, parents, and agencies in the larger community to support students' learning and well-being.

Find out why and how these principles were developed.

PROFESSIONAL ETHICS

What are your rights and responsibilities as a future teacher and current student teacher? A good teacher focuses on students and provides a safe environment for learning. The NEA (National Education Association) Code of Ethics adopted by the 1975 Representative Assembly serves as a guide for all teachers.

The preamble states, "The educator, believing in the worth and dignity of each human being, recognizes the supreme importance of the pursuit of truth, devotion to excellence, and the nurture of democratic principles." The Code of Ethics includes two major principles: Commitment to the Student and Commitment to the Profession. Both are based on striving to reach the highest potential. Visit the NEA website (http://www.nea.org/) to read the entire code.

1. What did you learn from reading the Code of Ethics?

2. List any ethical situations that come to mind as you begin student teaching.

3. Interview your cooperating teacher about his or her view of ethics and the profession of teaching. Ask the teacher what his or her perspective is on ethics in his or her classroom and in the school.

4. Discuss ethics with your supervisor. Review the NEA Code of Ethics and talk about any areas that may be confusing to you at this time.

ACT
Process 1.8   How Does the Law Relate to Me?

THE LAW AND STUDENT TEACHING

You will need to know your legal rights, responsibilities, and liabilities as a student teacher and future teacher. Talk with your school site cooperating teacher and principal to become knowledgeable about local and state laws that govern your student teaching experience. If there is an education law course offered at your college, you may want to meet with the professor to obtain current information. Information is also available on the Internet and in the books located in the CONNECT section of this chapter.

1. Review the laws for the following and understand how they relate to teaching:

   ☐ Discipline (corporal punishment in your state)

   ☐ Negligence (parents, guardians, or in classroom)

   ☐ Child abuse (emotional, physical, sexual—how to report)

   ☐ Handicapped Children and IDEA Individuals with Disabilities Act (Public Laws 94-142 and 101-476)

   ☐ Individualized education program (IEP) required

   ☐ Liability insurance (What is it? Do you need it?)

   ☐ Search and seizure (drugs, weapons, and obscene materials)

   ☐ Self-defense and excessive force (How are they defined?)

   ☐ Copyright laws (Internet, hard copy—what is fair use for teaching?)

   ☐ First aid and medications (Who is responsible for giving to students?)

   ☐ Academic freedom (censorship, banning books, religious issues)

   ☐ Personal life (what you do when you are not teaching)

2. Interview the building principal or school guidance counselor about issues that relate to state and federal laws.

3. What are your rights and responsibilities as a student teacher?

ACT
Process 1.9   What Do I Believe about Teaching and Learning?
Assumptions, Beliefs, and Dispositions

As you begin your student teaching, you have an opportunity to think about what you believe about teaching. This process relates in many ways to Process 1.1, *Why Did I Choose Teaching?* Take some time to think about the following and share your thoughts with your supervisor.

- Write three words that come to mind that describe how you feel right now as you enter student teaching.

    1. _____ 2. _____ 3. _____

    Other feelings: _____

    _____

    _____

- Write two assumptions you have about teachers.

    1. _____

    _____

    _____

    _____

    2. _____

    _____

    _____

    _____

- Write one core belief you bring to this experience.

    I believe _____

    _____

    _____

    _____

    _____

Use these to deepen your understanding of what *you* bring to the practicum. Compare and share with other student teachers.

STUDENT TEACHING REQUIREMENTS

1. Talk with your supervisor to review which national and state guidelines will guide your program.

2. State competencies vary but most agree that teachers need to have a command of subject matter knowledge. They also need to be able to:

   a. Plan Curriculum and Instruction

   b. Deliver Effective Instruction

   c. Manage Classroom Climate and Operations

   d. Assess Student Learning

   e. Promote Equity

   f. Meet Professional Responsibilities

3. College requirements vary; some include seminars, courses with practica, or other activities. Most teacher education programs include the following:

   a. Text- and field-related readings

   b. Field experience

   c. Journal reflections

   d. Attendance at on-campus events

   e. Course or seminar taken with student teaching

   f. Student teaching binder or portfolio

4. Student teachers are invited guests in practicing teachers' classrooms. They should follow the NEA Code of Ethics and be professional members of the teaching community. Teaching professionalism is evidenced in the following behaviors:

   a. Professional dress at the school site

   b. Consistent attendance and procedure for making up days lost to illness or weather

   c. Arrival time/departure: come early and stay later to prepare all lessons

   d. Self-motivation: ask questions, volunteer to help, initiate ideas and sharing

   e. Confidentiality: children's records, subject of meetings with parents, and so on, are not to be repeated outside of school

   f. Professional communication with parents, students, and other teachers

5. Ask your supervisor to share any other professional standards your teacher preparation program may be guided by this semester.

Most student teaching programs require a student teaching portfolio at the end of the practicum. This serves as evidence of completion of the program as well as demonstrates progress over time. A student teaching portfolio is a competency portfolio to demonstrate course standards have been met, as opposed to a presentation portfolio highlighting strengths for a potential employer (Chapter 10).

Tips from Former Student Teachers

1. **Get Started Early!** Don't wait until the end of the student teaching semester to organize materials for your portfolio. Begin the first week!

2. **Review the University Standards** Make sure you are clear about what needs to be assessed at the end of your experience and label each document that relates to the standards required.

3. **Collect Artifacts throughout the Semester** Collect everything you think might be useful—samples of student work illustrating achievement, ways you modified lessons, sample lesson plans, discipline strategies, and so on. Get a crate or file box and drop materials into folders clearly labeled by standard requirement.

4. **Document Classroom Organization** Draw diagrams and take photos of different ways in which you organized (or your teacher organized) the classroom. Write a rationale explaining the space organization in the room.

5. **Take Photographs** Keep a camera in your classroom to document special projects, student work, bulletin boards, and so on. Make sure you get permission to take photos of students.

6. **Collect Lesson Plans and Units** You don't usually need *all* your plans in your culmination portfolio. Follow guidelines from your university and select samples of lessons and units that demonstrate your competency in daily and long-range planning.

7. **Summarize Your Inquiry** Reread all your journals and reflect on your experience. Write a short summary to include in your portfolio that illustrates your growth and development from beginning to end.

Add any other tips to your list!

A very important aspect of becoming a professional is looking like one. Before you enter the school building, review the dress codes with your university faculty. Even if the teachers at the school dress casually, it is better for you as a beginning teacher to dress more formally.

The quickest way to distinguish yourself as a teacher to students is to "look" like a teacher. Remember, you will be observing for a few days/weeks and the students will be observing you too!

- What is the dress code at your student teaching school? Do the students have a dress code? If there is no formal dress code what are the expectations for teachers?

- How do you think professional dress relates to setting professional boundaries with students?

- What do you need to do to prepare your professional dress for student teaching?

- Review all dress codes with your university supervisor prior to visiting the school. Also talk with the cooperating teacher the first day to make sure you are interpreting the dress code appropriately.

REFLECT

Three ways you may use to reflect on your practice during student teaching are listed on this page. Select the methods of reflection that will stimulate your thinking. Write in an *Inquiry Journal* during student teaching. This writing will serve as a data source for solving problems over time. Uncover your own assumptions, biases, and dispositions as you write in your journal several times each week.

✓ **Inquiry: Teacher Research as a Tool for Solving Classroom Problems and Enhancing Student Learning**

What questions are arising as you begin your practicum experience? What assumptions are you making about students, parents, families, and schools?

_____

_____

_____

Review the *Key Questions* in the PLAN section of this chapter. Which questions are still confusing? List them below and set up a time to discuss them with your cooperating teacher or supervisor.

_____

_____

_____

_____

✓ **Self-Reflection: Analyze Your Teaching Strategies to Enhance Student Learning** (Use the processes in Chapter 1 to guide your self-reflection.)

Why did you decide to become a teacher? What are your goals?

_____

_____

_____

_____

✓ **Critique: Feedback from Your Supervisor and Cooperating Teacher to Guide Your Planning, Instructional Practice, and Professionalism**

When have you last received feedback about your teaching? What was your reaction? How did you use the information to improve your practice?

_____

_____

_____

_____

NOTES

Keep track of your ideas, thoughts, and things to do by writing them here.

Chapter 2

Getting Started at the School

Where Do I Begin?

Observe as many teachers and students as you can during your practicum. Many variables exist in the world of education. You will see students who are new, old, immature, mature, disruptive, silent, smart, struggling, stable, and unsure. You will see teachers who are new, old, secure, insecure, conforming, nonconforming, professional, unprofessional, skeptical, and nurturing. It is amazing to see teachers use many strategies with different classes and levels. Observing allows us to see how things work and more importantly why.

Student Teacher

Beginning the student teaching experience at the school site is exciting. Taking careful steps from the beginning of the experience creates positive first impressions and also gives you the foundation you need to build a strong experience. Three important aspects of getting started at the school site include (1) introducing yourself to many important people, (2) observing to learn about the school and its teachers, and (3) designing a plan for your practicum experience.

The school culture has been established over many years of operation and relationship building among staff members. There may be a new principal or this leader may have been a leader at the school for many years. As a student teacher coming into a new setting, you will need to be observant of the social structures that exist around you. Remember, you are a guest in a school that has been willing to welcome and host a beginning teacher. You are not part of the full-time faculty, even though it is advantageous to take on the role of teacher as often as possible. Establishing relationships with your cooperating teacher as well as many other teachers and educational support staff is vital to your success as a student teacher. Introducing yourself to the department chairperson, the secretaries, and other professional staff members—such as counselors, school nurse, school psychologist, bilingual teachers, special education teachers, and custodians—is a necessary part of integrating into an existing school setting.

Before "jumping in," observe carefully and listen to others as they talk about the school. Is this a positive place for teachers? What are the difficult issues? How do teachers interact with the principal? How does the school "feel" to you? These questions can be documented in your journal or can be part of the CONNECT conversations you might have throughout the semester.

In some cases, you may work with more than one cooperating teacher, especially if you are in a team situation or if you are part of a high school department. In this case, you should work with the department chair to identify the one teacher who will be signing your paperwork and who will serve as your cooperating teacher. Clearly, it is an advantage to be able to work with more than one teacher because you will be able to observe several teaching styles as you discover your own.

You should meet with your college supervisor during the first week of your student teaching for a "kick-off" meeting that will review all the requirements for student teaching. You should bring your practicum syllabus and any other materials you received from the college along with your questions. This meeting is often held with other student teachers who will be working with this university supervisor and can serve as an opportunity for you to connect with other student teachers who will be in the field. Continuing these meetings throughout the semester can serve as support for you and other student teachers, whether your supervisor attends or not.

If you are taking a course or seminar along with student teaching, be sure to read the syllabus and stagger your assignments wherever possible. Courses are designed to support your work in the classroom and to promote inquiry into your teaching. Use them to enhance your experience and deepen your reflection about teaching and learning. It is important to stay on schedule with any readings and to start early in the semester with your assignments, because as you move toward full-time teaching you will be extremely busy every night preparing lessons.

One of the keys to having a successful student teaching experience is being organized and focused on the task at hand. Meeting the people in the first week who will serve as your coaches, observing the school culture, and preparing a thoughtful plan for the experience are all important aspects of getting started on the right foot.

Discussing Professional Standards

National standards guide new teacher preparation in the United States. The INTASC created 10 principles for effective teaching. These principles are offered to you as a way to focus your attention on these key elements of practice. The "bottom line" is all about student learning. Are your students learning? How do you know?

Use these pages in each chapter to frame a quality conversation with your cooperating teacher and university supervisor. Don't be afraid to ask your own questions, too. Also use the REFLECT pages at the end of each chapter to deepen your thinking and to continue your quality conversations throughout the practium experience and into your first year of teaching.

INTASC Principles

Focus for Chapter 2

Discuss:
Principle #10   The teacher fosters relationships with school colleagues, parents, and agencies in the larger community to support students' learning and well-being.

Review:
Principle #9   The teacher is a reflective practitioner who continually evaluates the effects of his or her choices and actions of others (students, parents, and other professionals in the learning community) and who actively seeks out opportunities to grow professionally.

ASK YOURSELF   What do these principles mean to me right now? How will I know if I have achieved these principles?

DISCUSS WITH YOUR SUPERVISOR
OR COOPERATING TEACHER:

How will your supervisor/cooperating teacher know if you have achieved these principles? What evidence will you have to demonstrate these skills to them?

How will you know if your students have learned as a result of your teaching?

PLAN

USE ADVICE FROM FORMER STUDENT TEACHERS

Talk to student teachers who have just completed the experience and review the tips below to guide you.

- Be flexible as you plan your practicum, especially as you try to integrate requirements from the university into existing curriculum.
- Schedule time to observe other student teachers, other cooperating teachers, and specialty teachers in your school. Plan now!
- Get to know the whole school and the neighborhood in which you are teaching. Your students will appreciate your efforts in getting to know who they are and where they live.
- Ask questions! Write them down and keep track of what you need to know about teaching, learning, and the structure of schools.

PROCESS YOUR EXPERIENCE

Respond to the Key Questions below by completing the process pages in each chapter. These ACTs will encourage you to deepen your thinking about teaching and learning. Write on the pages and save them to review at the end of the experience.

KEY QUESTIONS

1. Who do I need to know at the school?

2. What can I learn about the community, the school, and my classroom?

3. How should I organize my practicum plan?

PLAN

TAKE CARE OF YOURSELF AND AVOID STRESS

Plan to avoid the typical stresses of student teaching by following advice from cooperating teachers and university supervisors.

GET UP EARLY!

To reduce stress it is important to plan your day. Get up 30 minutes earlier than you need to and organize your day. Be on time to school so you can start the day in a calm, refreshing manner. Your attitude every day makes a difference in your stress level.

What time will you have to get up to have 30 extra minutes each morning?

Some students prefer to stay 30 minutes at the end of the day to leave the list on their desk. You should still get up at least 15 minutes earlier in the morning so you come in refreshed and not "running" from your commute. Being on time or early creates a positive impression.

PLAN YOUR WEEK

Priority List

Done	Tasks	Priority	Complete by When?

Place things to do on the day you would like to do them.

Monday Date:	Tuesday Date:	Wednesday Date:	Thursday Date:	Friday Date:

CONNECT

CONNECT is a resource page with ideas and suggestions to support you during student teaching. Select and complete any CONNECT items that will enhance your experience in the classroom.

CONNECT with people

- Teachers
  Interview one or more teachers to find out why they chose this profession.
- Other educational support personnel (nurse, custodian, secretary, etc.)
  Ask several other people what they see as the strengths of this school.
- Students
  Ask students what they like best about this school.

CONNECT with readings & resources

- Curriculum materials
  Collect and read all curriculum materials you will be teaching.
- School policies and procedures
  Review school policies and procedures as written in the school handbook.
- Books and authors to explore on the Internet or at your local library
  Authors to explore: Eleanor Duckworth, Vivian Paley, Shirley Brice Heath, Beverly Tatum, Roland Barth
  Teacher's Survival Guide by Warner and Bryan (Park Avenue)
  The Student Teacher's Handbook by Schwebel (Erlbaum Associates)

CONNECT technology to teaching

- Explore and discover websites to visit and use in your classroom. Try these:
  Teacher Talk = http://educ.indiana.edu/cas/tt/v2i2/cultural.html
  Telling Stories = http://www.teachingeducation.com/vo19-labs-craig.htm
  Education World = www.educationworld.com
  My Virtual Reference Desk = http://www.refdesk.com
- Bookmark new sites you discover!
- Ask and observe how teachers use technology in their classrooms at this school.

ACT
Process 2.1 Creating a School Profile
What Is the School Culture?

Some of this information may be on file in your college Office of Practicum Experiences. Check there and with your local school's office. Many schools have webpages, too! This information can be used in your teaching portfolio for the job search.

Name of School:_____

Principal: _____

School Secretary(ies):_____

Custodian:_____

Departments (high school):_____

Address: _____

_____

_____

Community (obtain map and note towns nearby):_____

Community Resources (people and places): _____

School Hours: _____

Recess:_____

Lunch:_____

Phone:_____

E-mail: _____

Voice-Mail System: _____

Public Transportation Near?_____

Population of the School:

  Number of Students: _____

  Diversity:_____

  Languages:_____

Special Focus Area or Theme for School:_____

Number of Classrooms: _____

Organization of Classrooms in School (draw or attach a floor plan)

Grade-Level Teachers for Each Grade:_____

Special Area Teachers:_____

Bilingual Programs:_____

Special Education Program

   Inclusion _____   **Pull-out**_____

Other Special Programs Offered:_____

Parent Involvement: _____

Other: _____

General Impression of the School:_____

ACT
Process 2.2 First Impressions
Meeting My Cooperating Teacher

CHECKLIST

_____ Collect the written consent form from college that your cooperating teacher agrees to host you. Return form to college.

_____ Deliver all materials from college that explain roles and responsibilities.

_____ Share your student teacher profile and résumé with courses you have taken.

_____ Interview cooperating teacher.

Sample questions:

1. How many years have you been teaching? In this area? At this school?

2. Why did you become a teacher? A cooperating teacher?

3. What do you see as the strengths of this class/school/community?

4. What will your expectations be for me?

5. How can I assist you in creating this as a positive experience?

_____ Ask your cooperating teacher to suggest a student you could interview.

_____ Discuss possible items for your "teacher survival packet" (ACT Process 2.6 in this chapter).

_____ Ask for copies of books you will be using so you can read ahead.

_____ Confirm start date, end date, and school vacation days.

_____ Exchange phone numbers and establish appropriate call times.

_____ Set up first meeting with supervisor and cooperating teacher.

_____ Ask your questions.

_____ Other _____

ACT
Process 2.3 Other Important People
Who Is Watching Me?

- College supervisor name:_____ Phone:_____
  Questions for the college supervisor:

- Cooperating teacher name: _____ Phone:_____
  Questions for the cooperating teacher:

- Building Principal or Headmaster
  (Thank this person for allowing you to student teach at this school.)
- Department Chair (for middle school or high school student teachers)

  Name:_____ Phone:_____

- Other teachers in the building
    Grade-level team members
    Department teachers in subject areas
    Art, music, and physical education teachers
    Bilingual teachers
- Specialists in the building
    School nurse
    School security officer
    Psychologist
    Counselor
- Educational support personnel
    Secretaries
    Aides
    Custodians
- Student teachers
    From your college
    From other local colleges
- Parents
    Volunteers
    Organizations
- Other important people

ACT
Process 2.4   Initial Three-Way Conference

WHO: The "Student Teaching Triad" (you, your cooperating teacher, and your college supervisor). The college supervisor facilitates the meeting with opportunity for all to ask questions.

WHAT: Meeting to review requirements and plan the student teaching experience.

WHERE: At the school site.

WHEN: Usually the first or second week of student teaching.

WHY: To prepare for a successful student teaching experience!

SAMPLE AGENDA

1. Introductions
   - Discuss the role(s) each person in the triad will play during the experience.
   - Have the cooperating teacher share her or his expectations and how she or he views her or his role.
2. Cooperating Teacher Orientation
   - Policies and procedures
   - Syllabus, requirements, certification competencies
   - Benefit to accepting student (i.e., course voucher)
   - Handbook of techniques and strategies
3. Documentation of Experience
   - Forms—how and when
4. Supervision Procedures (see Chapter 3)
5. Questions from Cooperating Teacher
6. Nuts and Bolts
   - Beginning and ending dates noted
   - Dress code
   - Attendance procedures
   - Substitute teacher policy (check college guidelines regarding this)
   - Setting up first observation visit

This letter's style will vary depending on the age level of the students. Primary students could receive a large "big book"–style letter; older students could have a more formal, traditional letter form. The cooperating teacher should share the letter with the students before the student teacher arrives.

Date: _____

Dear Students,

My name is _____ and I will be student teaching with Mrs. Jones for the next x weeks. I am completing my senior year at University College with a double major of history and education. I have taken several exciting courses in archeology, and I thought it would be interesting to share this information with you.

I have traveled to several different parts of the United States, and I collect artifacts of Native Americans, particularly Southwestern Indians. I hope to design several history lessons that relate to this topic.

I decided to become a teacher because I like my subject area and enjoy sharing it with others. I've taught museum programs for students and summer YMCA extension courses already.

Mrs. Jones and I will be working together to make this a positive learning experience for all of you. I look forward to meeting you next Monday.

Sincerely,

Student Teacher

Date: _____

Dear Parents,

Our class is very fortunate to have _____ (name of student teacher) from Higher Education College join us as he begins his student teaching. The Anytown Public Schools have always been involved in the preparation of teachers, and this is another opportunity for our school and classroom to experience the enthusiasm of a beginning professional teacher.

Having a student teacher participate in our classroom allows the students to experience a variety of teaching methods. It also provides our classroom with two teachers so that more individual attention may be given to the students. Many of the lessons will be co-taught with me. Please be assured that I will be working cooperatively with _____ and that all that activities and lessons will be supervised by me. If you have any questions, do not hesitate to call me. _____ will be attending our school "Open House" next week. Please join me in welcoming him to our staff for the fall term.

Sincerely,

Cooperating Teacher

_____ (name of student teacher)

Process 2.6A Getting to Know the School— Creating a Survival Packet

Sample Survival Items

With the assistance of your cooperating teacher and the school secretary, you should begin to compile important materials that will assist you throughout the practicum. The following checklist will guide you.

SAMPLE SURVIVAL ITEMS

☐ School and student handbooks with mission statements and policies

☐ Curriculum guides and textbooks with teacher editions

☐ Daily schedules

☐ Class lists and seating charts for students and faculty list of teachers and other staff

☐ Fire drill and building evacuation procedures

☐ Students with special needs or health issues (e.g., first aid and medications)

☐ Sample of report card and progress reports

☐ Map of school with room numbers for location of copy room, rest rooms, faculty room, and library

☐ Policies for communicating with parents—any special forms required

☐ Discipline policies for school and classroom—written and informal procedures

☐ Guidelines for referring students to principal—forms and expectations

☐ Supervisory duties during the school day—Cafeteria? Hall duty? Study hall?

☐ Policies for reporting child abuse, neglect, and other legal issues—state laws

☐ Professional development opportunities during student teaching

☐ At-risk students—how they are supported

☐ Other

☐ Other

ACT
Process 2.6B Getting to Know the School— Creating a Survival Packet
Buzzwords I Need to Know

As you observe and get started, find the definitions to the following common school terms. Review your teacher education courses or ask your cooperating teacher, principal, or university supervisor to share the answers with you. Write any additional buzzwords below.

AFDC

AFT

Assertive discipline

At-risk students

Authentic assessment

Behavior modification

Block schedule

Bloom's taxonomy

Classified personnel

Compensatory education

Core curriculum

Cumulative folder

Curriculum frameworks

Evaluation (teacher)

Heterogeneous

Holistic scoring

Homogeneous

IEP

In-service education

Integrated curriculum

KWL

Least restrictive environment

NEA

Networking

Prep time

Professional status

Specials

Split class

Tenure

Tracking

Whole language

ACT
Process 2.7 Getting to Know the Students
Setting Professional Boundaries

As a beginning teacher, you will be tempted to become friends with your students. You will want them to like you and you will want to like them. After all, you have been looking forward to teaching and you have lots to offer students!

If you are teaching elementary and early childhood education, it will be obvious to your students that you are another adult in the classroom. However, if you are in middle school or secondary education, you may be close in age to the students you will be teaching. They may try to be your friend. This can confuse you if they ask you personal questions or cross boundaries with you.

- If a student says: Can I talk to you privately and will you promise not to tell anyone what I am telling you? I trust you more than my teacher.

                                    . . . just say NO!

  You have no idea what the student will say to you and if you are legally bound to tell authorities.

- If a student says: Can you come to my house to help me study tonight? My parents won't be home and I need extra help. You are the only one who understands me.

                                    . . . just say NO!

  You should not go to any student's home without their parents present. Suggest that the student stay after school with you in the library or a classroom that is supervised.

- If a student says: Can you give me a ride home? My bike is broken (my car broke down, I missed the bus, etc.).

                                    . . . just say NO!

  You should not give any student a ride in your car. Offer to assist the student in finding a way home.

Discuss other possible "boundary-crossing" dilemmas you may find yourself in during student teaching with your cooperating teacher and supervisor.

Don't be tempted to cross a professional boundary!

Get to know the community of the school district and near the school. This will help you understand your students and their families. You may be student teaching in another part of the country that is unfamiliar to you. Don't make assumptions about students, families, and the community without investigating and learning about them.

THE NEIGHBORHOOD NEAR THE SCHOOL

It is important to know the neighborhood in which you are student teaching. Are students walking to school or are they bused in from other parts of the city or county? Can you walk the neighborhood or are you teaching in a rural area?

List descriptive qualities of the neighborhood.

THE PROFESSIONAL COMMUNITY OF THE SCHOOL/DISTRICT/CITY/TOWN

Who are the important people in the school who govern the professional community? How are decisions made? Who is the superintendent? Who sits on the School Committee or the Town Council governing the school?

How does the professional community impact your school? Are there resources or people you should connect with during student teaching?

COMMUNITY RESOURCES

What are the resources offered in your town/city? Is there a library? Do your students have library cards? Art museum? Resource Center?

Name the local resources near the school. Use them!

ACT
Process 2.9A   Observing My Cooperating Teacher

WHAT ARE YOU LOOKING FOR WHEN YOU OBSERVE A TEACHER?

1. How the teacher manages the classroom:
    Physical organization of classroom
    Pacing of lesson
    Beginning and ending of lesson
    Monitoring of students
    Traffic flow of classroom
    Routines and procedures used
    Structure of lesson

2. Which instructional strategies are used during the lesson:
    Instructional practices used—Lecture? Cooperative? Combination?
    Teaching materials and audiovisual
    Technology use incorporated into lesson

3. How the classroom environment is organized and executed:
    Teacher's "style"—How would you describe it?
    Interactions with students
    Engagement of students with diverse needs
    Positive reinforcement
    Disruptions—How are they handled?

4. How the lesson was planned as part of a larger curriculum:
    The lesson plan—Was there one?
    The plan as part of a unit—How does this fit into the bigger picture?
    Curriculum objectives for learning—Clear?

5. How the lesson was assessed for learning:
    Formal assessment
    Informal assessment

6. How will you document your observations? Select one or more.
    a. Taking notes and responding to the questions listed above.
    b. Drawing a diagram of the classroom and noting interactions on paper.
    c. Audiotaping the lesson and responding to tape and comparing to notes taken.
    d. Writing a general summary in your journal.

ACT
Process 2.9B   Observing My Cooperating Teacher

Teacher: _____   **Subject:** _____   **Time:**_____

Teacher #2 (if co-teaching): _____

1. **Classroom management/routines.** How is the classroom organized? *Sketch a class-room setup and attach to this observation.* Do any special features of classroom management/teacher routines stand out for you? Passing out papers? Attendance? and so on. What special materials are in the classroom? Computers? Student areas? Mailboxes? Posters?

2. **Class start.** How does the class begin? Housekeeping activities? Calendar? What else? How long does this take? Time_____.

3. **Lesson purpose/objective.** Exactly how does the lesson begin? What is the transition between starting rituals and the content of the lesson. How are directions and overall objectives/goals of lesson shared with students?

4. **Procedure for lesson.** What is the sequence of activities in the lesson? List each type of activity/task here with time taken to complete each one.

Type of Activity (lecture, group work, etc.)	Time Spent

5. **Teaching for understanding.** How does the teacher know if the students understand what she or he is teaching? Does the teacher use any assessment instruments to evaluate student progress? List them.

6. **Effectiveness of lesson for diverse learners**. What was the most effective part of the lesson in your opinion? Were there any special materials used? Was technology used? Audiovisuals? Props? How did these assist diverse learners?

7. **Behavior management.** How did the teacher handle any disruptive students? Students who were not listening?

8. **Closure of a lesson/class period.** How does the lesson end? Does the class period end when the lesson ends? If not, what happens between the lesson ending and the period ending?

9. **Students' reaction to the lesson.** What did you observe generally? Were all students listening? Learning? What evidence do you have for this impression? If you asked a student what the purpose of this lesson was, what would he or she say?

10. **Modifications of the lesson.** If you were asked to teach this same lesson, what would you do? Add? Delete? Use other materials? How would these changes enhance student learning?

What is your overall impression of the lesson?

Questions for the cooperating teacher(s). What would you like to know more about?

ACT
Process 2.9C Observing My Cooperating Teacher to Create a Lesson Plan

Fill in the lesson plan with words and phrases that "create" the cooperating teacher's lesson plan.

Talk with the cooperating teacher after the lesson observation to compare and share what you observed.

Subject:_____ **Date:**_____

OBJECTIVES

1. _____

_____

2. _____

_____

3. _____

_____

Key Vocabulary	
1. _____	4. _____
2. _____	5. _____
3. _____	6. _____

Key Questions
1. _____
2. _____
3. _____

Materials/Resources/Technology

Procedure (Beginning, Middle, Closing)

Assessment

Classroom Management Notes/Lesson Modifications

Homework/Follow-up/Enrichment

ACT
Process 2.9D Observing My Cooperating Teacher to Document the Lesson Plan

Observe the cooperating teacher. Write the lesson plan you think the cooperating teacher used to teach this lesson. Meet with the cooperating teacher after the lesson and compare your observations and impressions with what the teacher intended to teach.

LESSON PLAN

1. **Purpose of the lesson**

   Why is the teacher teaching this lesson?

2. **Goals and expected learning objectives**

   What is the teacher expecting to achieve in this class period? Key questions? Key vocabulary?

3. **State curriculum frameworks/school curriculum focus areas**

   How does the teacher's plan relate to other curriculum standards?

4. **Materials and technology**

   What does the teacher use to promote interest and student learning?

5. **Procedure/activities for the lesson**

   How does the teacher organize his or her time to meet the objectives? What did the teacher plan for the students who finished early?

6. **Assessments/evaluation of student learning**

   What did the teacher use informally or formally to measure whether students learned? What modifications were made for diverse learners?

7. **Homework/enrichment**

   What is required or encouraged?

ACT
Process 2.9E   Observing an Individual Student

Date:_____   First Name of Student: _____

Grade/Subject:_____

1. What do you notice about this student (physical appearance, cultural background, language, social interaction, skills and abilities, motivation, attitude, self-concept, etc.)?

2. How is the student responding to the teacher's lesson?

3. Is the student interacting with any other students? Describe.

4. What is the quality of the student's work?

5. Name something positive the student did during the lesson.

6. What other things did you observe?

ACT
Process 2.9F   Observing Large Group Dynamics

Class Period: _____ **Time of Day:**_____

Grade Level/Subject Observed: _____ **Date:**_____

1. Sketch the classroom and how students are seated. Attach to this form for future discussions. How does class seating impact the lesson? The students' behavior?

2. How would you describe the group dynamics of the students in this class? How do they relate to each other? How do they relate to the teacher?

3. Can you notice any individual learning differences among students? What makes you say this? How might this impact the group dynamic in this class?

4. Are there cliques in this class? Who are the leaders, academic or social? Is there a need for any student to receive attention from the teacher or peers?

5. Are any students excluded from classroom dynamics (for example, those who are bored, hostile, disengaged, doing another task, sleeping, etc.?) (Note: Use the sociogram in Chapter 4 to explore this further.)

6. In your opinion, what are some factors that are impacting the class dynamic?

Factor	*How It Is Impacting the Class Dynamic*
Teacher's lesson plan	
Seating arrangement/groups	
Attitude/behavior of students	
Teacher's expectation for learning	
Other adults in room	

ACT
Process 2.9G   Observing Small Groups

Class Period: _____   Time of Day:_____

Grade Level/Subject Observed: _____   Date:_____

GENERAL IMPRESSION OF SMALL GROUPS
AS PART OF A WHOLE CLASS LESSON

1. How were the groups chosen and why? Where are they located? Do students need to move to get into groups? How is this done?

2. How were instructions for group work given?

3. How does the teacher assist all the groups? Which group does the teacher assist first? Is there any reason for this? How does the teacher move around the room?

4. What is the teacher doing when he or she is not working with a group? How does the teacher monitor the groups to ensure on-task behavior?

OBSERVING ONE SMALL GROUP MORE CLOSELY

1. Why is this group working together? Who is the leader? Why?

2. Are all members of the group participating? How does participation vary? Is the group completing the task assigned effectively?

3. How will the group be assessed for successful completion of the task? Was this group successful in your opinion?

4. What is your overall impression of group observation?

ACT
Process 2.9H   Observing a Student Teacher

Name: _____ Class Period:_____ Time of Day:_____

Grade Level/Subject Observed: _____ Date:_____

PRECONFERENCE WITH STUDENT TEACHER

Ask to see the lesson plan before you observe.

Ask if the student teacher would like to see the observation after it is completed.

Ask if there is something the student teacher would like you to focus on.

Ask if the student teacher would like feedback on the lesson.

OBSERVATION

1. What is the purpose of the lesson? Expectations for students?

2. How did the lesson begin? Directions?

3. How are students responding to the lesson? If students are not responding, why do you think that is happening?

4. What area did the student teacher want you to focus on for this class? What did you observe?

5. What did the students learn in this class? Based on that answer, what should the next lesson be?

Compliment for the student teacher:

REFLECT

Three ways you may use to reflect on your practice during student teaching are listed on this page. Select the methods of reflection that will stimulate your thinking. Write in an *Inquiry Journal* during student teaching. This writing will serve as a data source for solving problems over time. Uncover your own assumptions, biases, and dispositions as you write in your journal several times each week.

✓ **Inquiry: Teacher Research as a Tool for Solving Classroom Problems and Enhancing Student Learning**

What questions are arising as you observe your teacher, walk around the school, talk with students, or think about teaching? What is the school culture? How do you know?

_____

_____

_____

_____

Review the *Key Questions* in the *PLAN* section of this chapter. Which questions are still confusing? List them below and set up a time to discuss them with your cooperating teacher or supervisor.

_____

_____

_____

_____

✓ **Self-Reflection: Analyze Your Teaching Strategies to Enhance Student Learning** (Use the processes in Chapter 3 to guide your self-reflection.)

When have you used self-reflection in the past? How did it work for you?

_____

_____

_____

✓ **Critique: Feedback from Your Supervisor and Cooperating Teacher to Guide Your Planning, Instructional Practice, and Professionalism**

How do you like to receive feedback? Think about this and share your preference with your supervisor and cooperating teacher(s).

_____

_____

_____

_____

Chapter 3

Supervision during Student Teaching

How Do I Grow and Develop during This Experience?

The most important part of the supervision relationship is communication. Write in your journal and use it to build a foundation with your university supervisor. Remember that relationships with either your supervisor or cooperating teacher involve give and take. Don't be afraid to share your ideas too.

Student Teacher

Supervision is a process in which you will participate during your student teaching experience. Through meetings, visits to the school, observations of your teaching, and a review of your requirements, the university supervisor will "supervise" your growth and development as a beginning teacher.

Supervision will be both formative and summative. This means that as you are forming and learning, you will be coached and supported in mastering the competencies of teaching. You will not be expected to "be a teacher" the first week you enter a classroom. You will be expected to learn, observe, model effective practice, think about what you would do differently, write, reflect, plan, and respond to coaching from both your cooperating teacher and university supervisor. The *formative* supervision period is preparing you for more formal evaluation. Formative supervision provides "practice" time—where you should try new ideas and strategies and assess your comfort level in teaching. Along with your own self-reflection, formative supervision will provide you with a focus on teaching competencies that need development. By paying attention to your own strengths and weaknesses you will be better prepared for meeting all the teaching competencies.

Practice is to formative supervision as test is to summative supervision. A *summative* meeting with your university supervisor usually involves an observation that has been selected to measure competencies and a summary of your progress in all requirements to date. The final grade from your practicum is the summative evaluation based on your supervision from the whole semester.

Note that your college supervisor wears two distinct hats in that she or he will serve as your coach during the formative phase of your teaching and will also be required to formally assess the completion of your practicum and teaching competencies. How the supervisor carries out his or her responsibilities may vary from college to college. Typically, the supervisor will work with your cooperating teacher to collect information about your daily work in the field, read and respond to your weekly journal entries, provide support for you throughout the practicum, and recommend a final "summative" grade or a pass/fail that will be part of your university transcript. Keep in mind the summative reports, whether at the midterm or final, are a "summary" of your progress to date and will also include *all* other requirements, such as lesson plans, completed journals, attendance in seminar classes, and student teaching binder. This means supervision is more than just a midterm or final observation of a lesson.

Your practicum supervision is completed in a "student teaching triad" in which you play a key role in self-assessing your progress and setting goals to develop your skills. The cooperating teacher serves as a practice coach who works side by side with you to provide you with on-the-spot feedback. Your university supervisor is a "visiting" coach who provides support and feedback during your formative stages and a final evaluator who observes your development from an outside perspective and checks on all other college requirements.

How the supervisor actually carries out the supervision responsibilities may vary slightly among college programs. Typically, there will be approximately six visits to the school site. These may include

Initial. During the first week to set the stage and explain what will happen

Informal visit. To give a formative response to a lesson and set goals for midterm

Midterm. To observe a lesson and provide a summative report to date with all requirements and how well they have been completed

Informal visit. To provide formative support in areas that may need focus

Final observation. To observe another lesson for summative report

Closeout meeting. Completion meeting with you to check paperwork, check requirements, and discuss final grade

In addition to the school site visits, your supervisor may meet with you privately or in small groups to discuss common issues of student teaching. He or she may also use e-mail to communicate with you and/or to respond to your journal. Your supervisor might have weekly office hours or prefer that you call when you have an issue to discuss. Find out which support system is available to you during this supervised experience. Each visit, conversation, and response to your journal is a guide to assist you in developing as a teacher.

Discussing Professional Standards

QUALITY CONVERSATIONS TO ENHANCE STUDENT LEARNING

National standards guide new teacher preparation in the United States. The INTASC created 10 principles for effective teaching. These principles are offered to you as a way to focus your attention on these key elements of practice. The "bottom line" is all about student learning. Are your students learning? How do you know?

Use these pages in each chapter to frame a quality conversation with your cooperating teacher and university supervisor. Don't be afraid to ask your own questions, too. Also use the REFLECT pages at the end of each chapter to deepen your thinking and to continue your quality conversations throughout the practium experience and into your first year of teaching.

INTASC Principles

Focus for Chapter 3

Review

Principle #9   The teacher is a reflective practitioner who continually evaluates the effects of his or her choices and actions of others (students, parents, and other professionals in the learning community) and who actively seeks out opportunities to grow professionally.

Principle #10   The teacher fosters relationships with school colleagues, parents, and agencies in the larger community to support students' learning and well-being.

ASK YOURSELF   What do these principles mean to me right now? How will I know if I have achieved these principles?

DISCUSS WITH YOUR SUPERVISOR OR COOPERATING TEACHER:

How will your supervisor/cooperating teacher know if you have achieved these principles? What evidence will you have to demonstrate these skills to them?

How will you know if your students have learned as a result of your teaching?

PLAN

USE ADVICE FROM FORMER STUDENT TEACHERS

Talk to student teachers who have just completed the experience and review the tips below to guide you.

- Encourage your cooperating teacher to give you feedback on your formal lessons. To make it easier, use the process form in this chapter and make multiple copies for him or her to use.
- Make sure you have a preconference with your supervisor and/or cooperating teacher prior to any observation. This lets you set the stage for the lesson and they can give you any last-minute advice before you begin.
- Schedule "talk time" with your cooperating teacher. This will put you in the teacher's very busy schedule at a regular time each week. Create a plan for each session so you know what to discuss. Make sure there is time for questions.

PROCESS YOUR EXPERIENCE

Respond to the Key Questions below by completing the process pages in each chapter. These ACTs will encourage you to deepen your thinking about teaching and learning. Write on the pages and save them to review at the end of the experience.

KEY QUESTIONS

1. Who are the key people supporting me during this experience?

2. What is supervision and how do I participate?

3. How do I solve problems during the practicum?

4. How do I connect my cooperating teacher/school to the college program?

PLAN

TAKE CARE OF YOURSELF AND AVOID STRESS

Plan to avoid the typical stresses of student teaching by following advice from cooperating teachers and university supervisors.

DRESS FOR SUCCESS!

How you look often affects how you feel in the classroom. Dress like a teaching professional and students will start to treat you that way. Your hair, cleanliness, nails, and general appearance are critical. Remember, you will have many people observing you informally or formally all day. Some schools have their own dress codes and others allow more informal dress. You should dress up as much as possible to demonstrate your professionalism. Talk with your cooperating teacher about any unwritten code expectations. You may need to purchase some professional clothing depending on the school code and culture.

What might you need to purchase?

PLAN YOUR WEEK

Priority List

Done	Tasks	Priority	Complete by When?

Place things to do on the day you would like to do them.

Monday Date:	Tuesday Date:	Wednesday Date:	Thursday Date:	Friday Date:

CONNECT

CONNECT is a resource page with ideas and suggestions to support you during student teaching. Select and complete any CONNECT items that will enhance your experience in the classroom.

CONNECT with people

- Teachers
  Interview your cooperating teacher about her own supervision for her job. If she has not been supervised for many years, talk with a beginning teacher at the school so you know what to expect when you become a first-year teacher.
- Principal
  Ask the principal or department chair which procedures she uses to supervise teachers in her building or department. How does this relate to your own supervision this semester?

CONNECT with readings & resources

- Videos and audiotapes
  Association of Supervision and Curriculum Development Videos (ASCD)
  Harry K. Wong Videotapes for beginning teachers (Wong)
- Books and authors to explore on the Internet or at your local library
  Teacher Self-Evaluation Tool Kit by Airasian and Gullickson (Corwin Press)
  Stories of Student Teaching by Pitton (Merrill-Prentice Hall)
  Student Teaching Casebook for Supervising Teachers by Wentz and Yarling (Merrill)
  A Handbook of Techniques and Strategies for Coaching Student Teachers by Pelletier
    (Allyn and Bacon)

CONNECT technology to teaching

- Check out these websites:
  The New York Times Learning Network = http://www.nytimes.com/learning/
  Planet Search = http://planetk-12.planetsearch.com
  Teacher Magazine = http://www.edweek.org/tm/
  http://www.teachnet.com
- Try electronic journal writing:
  Read the article in the *Journal of Computing in Teacher Education*, Vol. 10, no. 4.

ACT
Act Process 3.1   Who's Who? Roles and Responsibilities

The student teaching triad consists of the cooperating teacher, the student teacher, and the college supervisor. Each person plays a part in the development of a new teacher.

COLLEGE SUPERVISOR'S ROLE

Role: "Visiting coach"

_____ Responsible for providing overview of all requirements

_____ Responsible for providing support and guidance

_____ Responsible for giving feedback that promotes development

_____ Responsible for providing both formative and summative feedback in the context of supervision

_____ Responsible for "closeout" meeting with student teacher to review all requirements

_____ Responsible for preparing student for certification checkout meeting

_____ Responsible for modeling professional behavior

Ask your supervisor what other responsibilities he has and list them here:

COOPERATING TEACHER'S DAILY ROLE AND RESPONSIBILITIES

Role: Daily coach working side by side with you

_____ Responsible for welcoming you into her classroom

_____ Responsible for providing an environment for learning

_____ Responsible for working collaboratively with the college supervisor

_____ Responsible for offering suggestions and models for teaching

_____ Responsible for modeling professional behavior

Share this page with your cooperating teacher and ask her what other responsibilities she considers herself to have during this experience. List here:

STUDENT TEACHER'S ROLE

Role: "Prospective teacher"

_____ Responsible for completing all college requirements

_____ Responsible for attendance at school every day and making up any sick days

_____ Responsible for completing all certification requirements

_____ Responsible for 100 percent participation during practicum

_____ Responsible for accepting constructive feedback and implementing it

_____ Responsible for professionalism and confidentiality

List other responsibilities your supervisor and cooperating teacher believe are important to your development:

ACT
Process 3.2   What Is Supervision?

Supervision is the process of assessing your ability to become a practicing classroom teacher. Formal observation of your teaching is part of this process, and it usually takes place when your university supervisor visits to observe a lesson.

To formalize the process of observing, a clinical model is often used by university supervisors. This model includes a preconference, an observation of a lesson, and a postconference. Instructional practice clearly is an important part of your preparation and many aspects of your practice can be seen in the lessons you plan and teach. Please note, however, that all competencies are not observed in the clinical observation, and that is why conversations with your cooperating teacher and your journal entries are so important in developing all your teaching competencies. Carrying out a well-planned lesson clearly is important, but not at the expense of professionalism, communication, and subject matter knowledge.

You may want to invite your cooperating teacher to use this observation model any time she would like to formally review a lesson you are teaching. This allows her to view your teaching in a more organized way and also prepares you for your supervisor's visit.

PRECONFERENCE

A preconference is held prior to your actual teaching of a lesson. This may be a few minutes before you teach when you meet with your supervisor or cooperating teacher to share your plan for the lesson. A preconference does not have to take a long time, but it should not be skipped. It sets the stage for your lesson and gives the observer insights into your goals.

SAMPLE AGENDA FOR A PRECONFERENCE

1. Share the purpose of the lesson along with a detailed plan for assessing student progress.
2. Review how you will engage students in learning activities.
3. Ask your supervisor or cooperating teacher for any last-minute advice.
4. Discuss how your lesson will be observed (how data will be collected—see ACT Process 3.6).
5. Set up time for postconference.

OBSERVING THE LESSON

Your supervisor will select a technique for observing your teaching. Samples of possible ways in which supervisors observe are listed in ACT Process 3.6. The purpose of the observation is to agree on what you would like to see observed. The teaching competencies will serve as a guide for the supervisor, so you can expect the observation to focus on behaviors that relate to these.

SAMPLE AGENDA FOR A POSTCONFERENCE

1. Discuss how your expectations for the lesson compare to the reality.
2. Discuss data your supervisor collected.
3. Set goals for meeting competencies observed that need more attention.

ACT
Process 3.3   How Do I Like to Receive Feedback?

Accepting feedback is an important aspect of participating in a supervisory model. During student teaching there will be times when your "coaches" will either offer you suggestions or provide objective data for you to reflect on. Being open to this information will provide you with more of an opportunity to grow and develop as a teacher. Accepting feedback is not easy. Remind yourself of the situations in your life and how you typically respond, and then move through any difficult feedback sessions to see the growth ahead.

Answer the following questions and use the answers as a guide for you to think about how you will respond when you receive feedback. This exercise may also provide an awareness for you as you think about providing either direct or objective feedback to the students in your classes.

1. Think of a time you received feedback as a child. Describe the situation. Who gave you the feedback?

   Why do you think you recall this incident? What kind of feedback was it?

2. Think of a time recently that you received feedback. Describe the situation. Who gave you the feedback?

   Why do you think you recall this incident? What kind of feedback was it?

HOW DO YOU LIKE TO RECEIVE FEEDBACK?   Do you like feedback in writing so you can think about it? Do you like verbal comments at the end of the day? Describe your "feedback style":

Share with your supervisor and cooperating teacher how you like to receive feedback. Perhaps your "feedback preference" can be accommodated.

How will you know if you are growing as a teacher? How do you measure your progress against the professional standards and requirements for your student teaching course?

Meet with your university supervisor and discuss the "teaching behaviors" she is expecting to observe as you begin to prepare lessons and start teaching. What will she be observing when she comes to visit?

Review the INTASC principles if your teacher preparation program does not have its own performance standards. Make a list of specific "observable behaviors" and "documented evidences" that are examples of expected performance.

Complete the table and create your own for all the other principles!

INTASC Principle #3

The teacher understands how students differ in their approaches to learning and creates instructional opportunities that are adapted to diverse learners.

INTASC	Observable Behaviors	Documented Evidence
Principle #3	The student teacher uses a variety of teaching strategies during the observed lesson.	Lesson plans showed different strategies for different learners.
Principle #3	The student teacher uses higher-order thinking and question techniques during class discussion.	Questions were listed on the board during the lesson.
Principle #3	The student teacher organized part of the lesson in small groups with each group working at its own level.	Groups had different reading levels of the same content.
Principle #		
Principle #		
Principle #		
Principle #		

ACT
Process 3.5 Using a Performance
Rubric to Measure Progress

Create a performance rubric that matches your teacher preparation program standards. Measure your progress at midterm and when your complete your practicum. Make sure you are clear about what the "documented evidence" is that demonstrates you level of skill. Use the previous page to list examples of evidence that you should be striving to achieve as you grow.

Sample Rubric for INTASC Principle #3

The teacher understands how students differ in their approaches to learning and creates instructional opportunities that are adapted to diverse learners.

Examples of Documented Evidences	*Unsatisfactory* Have tried a number of times unsuccessfully 1	*Beginning* Just getting started 2	*Emerging* Have tried a few times with some success 3	*Applying* Demonstrates Competence and Confidence 4
Uses a variety of teaching strategies				
Uses Bloom's Taxonomy in designing lessons				
Manages small groups with varied instructional tasks				
Gives directions so all students understand what to do				
Provides differentiated instruction for learners				

SAMPLE OBSERVATION TECHNIQUES

Your supervisor and cooperating teacher may choose any of the following ways in which to collect data about your teaching or they may have one of their own. Ask at the preconference how the data will be collected when they are observing you teach.

_____ **Scripting** (Writing everything you say or do during the lesson. This is a profile of the lesson in narrative form.)

_____ **Verbal feedback** (Listening to your speaking as it relates to asking questions, giving praise, allowing talk time, reprimanding, or gender.)

_____ **Movement** (Recording how you move around the room or how students interact with you, or both.)

_____ **Timing** (Recording time it takes for introduction, giving directions, answering questions, doing assignments, cleaning up, etc.)

_____ **Audiotaping** (Providing equipment and taping you for voice, articulation, directions, or any specific aspect of speech.)

_____ **Videotaping** (Recording a lesson and observing the lesson together with nonjudgmental questions prepared.)

ACT
Process 3.7   Being Observed and Receiving Feedback

1. Review how you like to receive feedback and note that you may not always receive it that way. How will you respond? You may have to respond a new way. Remind yourself not to be defensive. Your coaches want you to be the best possible teacher, and the feedback is given to support that effort.

SUGGESTIONS FOR RECEIVING FEEDBACK

- Listen very carefully.
- Take notes.
- Ask questions to clarify what was said.
- Repeat back what the speaker said to get verification of what you heard.
- Clarify the feedback again if needed.
- Turn the feedback into a goal that relates to a teaching behavior.

Try not to take critical feedback personally!

2. Cooperating Teacher Feedback and Support
   - You may have to ask for feedback and support. If you ask, be prepared for answers. Ask your supervisor to assist with ideas for doing this at the initial three-way meeting you have at the beginning of the semester.
   - Set up a regular time that works for you and the cooperating teacher. It doesn't have to be a long time, but it should be consistent. Ten minutes every morning may be better for you than an hour at the end of the week; it depends on your schedules and time commitments. Work out a system that works for both of you.

3. Ask your supervisor how you will receive feedback about your ongoing development.

   Responses to journal entries

   Weekly seminars available for you to gain more support

   Verbal and written feedback after informal visits

   Written feedback after midterm and final observations

   Electronic connection—E-mail dialogue journals

   Group meetings with other student teachers

   Phone conversations

   Which of these do you prefer?

   List which ones you can expect during the semester after talking with your supervisor.

ACT
Process 3.8   Reflecting on Practice: The Inquiry Journal

One way to document your own thinking is to maintain an inquiry journal. Use the prompts at the end of each chapter on the REFLECT page or write about your own ideas.

SUGGESTIONS FOR WRITING IN YOUR JOURNAL

✓ Write at least two or three times a week to be able to document what is happening and what you think about what is happening.

✓ Don't use the journal as a diary or a log of what happened during the day. Instead, use it as a place for you to jot down questions you have, assumptions, dilemmas you are facing, or any situation that you may need to think more about.

✓ Some university programs require that journal entries be shared with the university supervisor. Use E-mail to send your journal! Make sure you check for spelling and grammar. Supervisors often respond and give you more questions and ideas to think about. Remember this is not about answers! It is about developing good questions!

✓ Use your journal to collect data on students that you are observing to enhance their learning. You may notice things that work during the day and you don't want to lose that thought!

✓ Reread your journal regularly to see how your thinking is changing. Be sure to read your journal at the end of the practicum to do a final reflection.

✓ Use inquiry to design teacher research questions that will assist you in solving your own classroom problems.

✓ You may want to create a "dialogue inquiry" with one or more student teachers. Simply start the dialogue on-line by asking a question or asking for assistance with a problem you are having. Let your partner respond! Keep all journals for future reference.

ACT
Process 3.9   Self-Evaluation—Completing
Course Requirements
How Am I Doing?

☐ College requirements
   Are they completed on time for supervisor review?
   Attending seminars?
   Completing thoughtful journal entries?
   Writing lesson plans and units?
   Student teaching binder complete?
   Other

Areas that I need to focus on are:

Goals with expected teaching behaviors:

☐ Fieldwork
   How well are my specific teaching behaviors matching teaching competencies?
   Implementation of lessons
   Design of units
   Classroom management
   Discipline
   Classroom assessment
   Other

Areas that I need to focus on are:

Goals with expected teaching behaviors:

ACT
Process 3.10 Self-Evaluation—Reviewing a Lesson Taught
What Are My Thoughts?

You may choose to self-evaluate by writing your thoughts on the lesson plans or attaching this form to each plan.

1. What did the students learn from this lesson? How do I know the students were actively engaged with the lesson?

2. How closely did I follow my lesson plan? Did I have to modify during the lesson? Why?

3. What do I think was the most effective part of the lesson?

4. Were the materials/visuals/aids appropriate? Why? Why not?

5. What would I change/keep the same the next time I do this lesson?

6. What do I see as my teaching strengths in these lesson?

7. A goal I would like to have my cooperating teacher assist me in reaching is . . .

ACT
Process 3.11   Self-Evaluation: Audio

Use audiotapes to *listen* to yourself in action. You will be surprised at how much you will learn about yourself as a teacher. A productive way to audiotape yourself teaching follows:

1. List two or three things you would like to listen for in the audiotape and write them down.
   Examples: my tone of voice, whether I call on all girls or boys, how I respond to student questions, how I give directions.

   _____

   _____

   _____

2. Listen to the tape.
   What did you hear related to these three areas?

   Ask yourself, "If I was a student in this class, would I be engaged in learning?"

   Sometimes there are unexpected surprises that you hear on the tape that you were not expecting. What did you notice?

   What else did you notice that could help you as a teacher?

Use these audiotapes as examples of how you give directions, how you lead a discussion, and how you close a classroom lesson. You could edit the tapes and create one tape that has your "best" examples of verbal teaching that could be used in your teaching portfolio.

ACT
Process 3.12   Self-Evaluation: Video

Videotaping is also a way to learn and observe yourself or your students. Audiotaping is recommended before attempting a videotape. This is *not* your teaching portfolio tape, but rather a way in which you can observe yourself and learn about your instructional practice. If you want to create a demonstration tape for your teaching portfolio later, you may do so. Let this tape be purely for your eyes only to give you information about your teaching.

TIPS FOR TAPING

1. Rather than taping yourself, focus the tape on the students in your classroom. You can learn a lot by watching how the students respond to your teaching!

2. Check with the cooperating teacher regarding taping permissions that may be required.

3. Follow the same guidelines for audiotaping and ask yourself two or three things you want to observe and focus on these.

4. What did you notice in the tape that you didn't expect?

Optional: You may want to view the tape with your cooperating teacher or university supervisor. One way is to view the tape side by side and ask your cooperating teacher to ask you probing questions throughout the viewing. Another way is to cue up the tape and share a portion of it and ask for feedback.

ACT
Process 3.13   Lesson Critique from Cooperating Teacher

You are encouraged to ask your cooperating teacher for feedback. Often, cooperating teachers give this information verbally, and student teachers may prefer it in writing so it can be reviewed later. This form is an easy way for the cooperating teacher to provide feedback on some of your lessons. Make several copies of this form and provide them for your cooperating teacher if she would like to use them.

FEEDBACK FORM

Date: _____   **Subject/Grade:**_____

Title of Lesson: _____

1. How well was the lesson plan written? Was it clear and easy to follow? Did it have a purpose that related to student learning?

2. How well did the student teacher carry out the lesson plan's objectives?

3. Describe one positive aspect of the lesson that demonstrates the student teacher's skills as a beginning teacher.

4. How were the students engaged during the lesson to encourage learning?

5. Commendations (positive aspects of teaching demonstrated):

6. Recommendations (suggestions for future lessons):

7. Other comments:

ACT
Process 3.14   Goal Setting to Focus and Improve Practice

GOAL SETTING

_____ 1. During the conference, jointly select one aspect where you can strive for growth. This could be a "recommendation" offered by the cooperating teacher or college supervisor.

_____ 2. Discuss specific actions you need to take to grow in this area. List those actions on this chart.

_____ 3. Set a time when you will review this plan to see if the goal has been met. At that time you may revise and continue with the same goal or select a new one and start the process again.

Goal	Actions	Evaluation
(State goal in measurable terms.)	(What will you do to achieve your goal?)	(Date for goal review. How will you know if you reached your goal?)

SAMPLE GOALS

Having interesting introductions to lessons, culminating a lesson in an orderly way, moving around the classroom, pronouncing all the words in a lesson correctly, managing an effective classroom routine during a lesson.

Make the goal achievable, observable, and measurable!

STUDENT TEACHER'S THOUGHTS

The next three pages include short reflective stems that will stimulate the thinking of all members of the student teaching triad. The "bubble sheets" have been nicknamed because they are short thoughts that come to mind. You may choose to complete as many thoughts as you wish weekly and use them as the basis for a longer journal entry. A "bubble sheet" gives you a chance to jot down things that "bubble" up during the course of the week and can serve as reminders for issues you would like to discuss in more depth.

Copy these forms each week and complete as many "bubbles" as you choose that apply to your situation that week.

COOPERATING TEACHER'S THOUGHTS

Invite your cooperating teacher to complete any of the "bubble sheet" prompts and use them in your weekly or daily discussions of your progress. Issues that may "bubble" up are often difficult for your cooperating teacher to raise verbally. This is an easy way to jot down an idea that can lead to a more in-depth discussion. These sheets can also assist the cooperating teacher in organizing his thoughts for the visits by the university supervisor. If "bubble sheets" are maintained weekly, they serve as a reminder of progress and will assist in the final recommendation letter the cooperating teacher is required to write.

SUPERVISOR'S THOUGHTS

Your supervisor may also want to complete a "bubble sheet" each time she visits during the semester or whenever she feels she has a "thought" about you and your teaching. It serves as a reminder for her about things she may want to discuss with you or the cooperating teacher in the future. It also documents many thoughts for the final summative report. These may also be shared at university supervisor meetings as a beginning of a discussion.

Bubble Sheet #1
Student Teacher's Thoughts

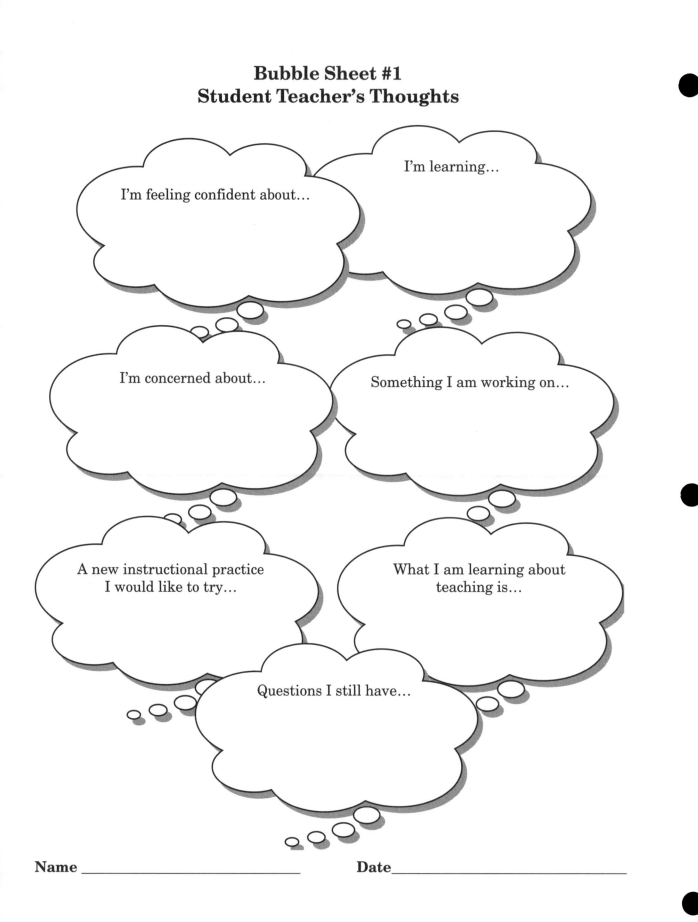

I'm feeling confident about...

I'm learning...

I'm concerned about...

Something I am working on...

A new instructional practice I would like to try...

What I am learning about teaching is...

Questions I still have...

Name _____   Date_____

Bubble Sheet #2
Cooperating Teacher's Thoughts

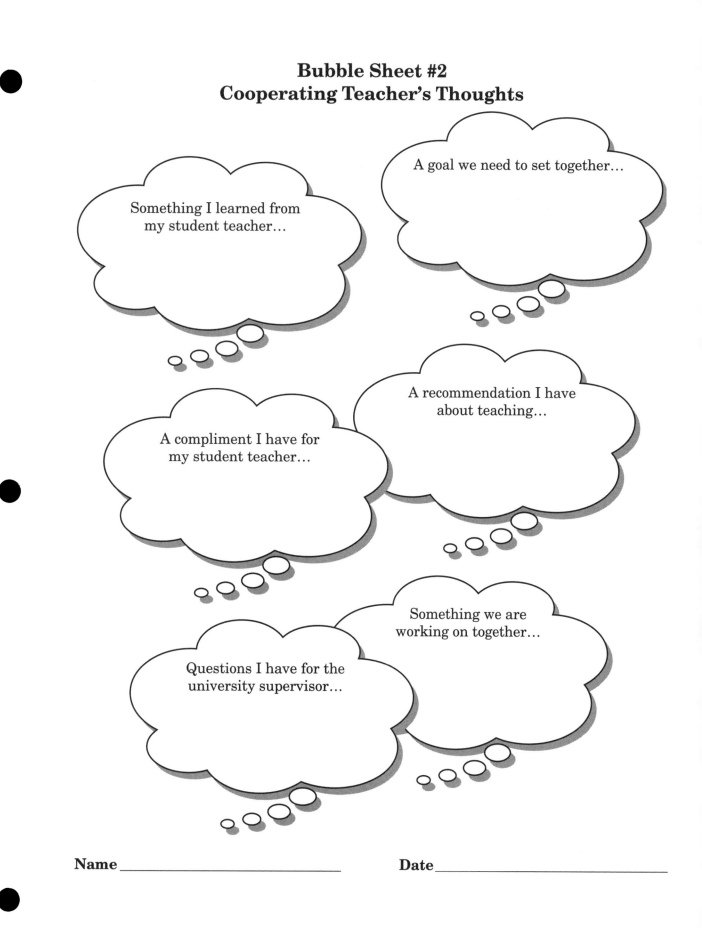

Something I learned from my student teacher…

A goal we need to set together…

A compliment I have for my student teacher…

A recommendation I have about teaching…

Questions I have for the university supervisor…

Something we are working on together…

Name _____   Date _____

Bubble Sheet #3
Supervisor's Thoughts

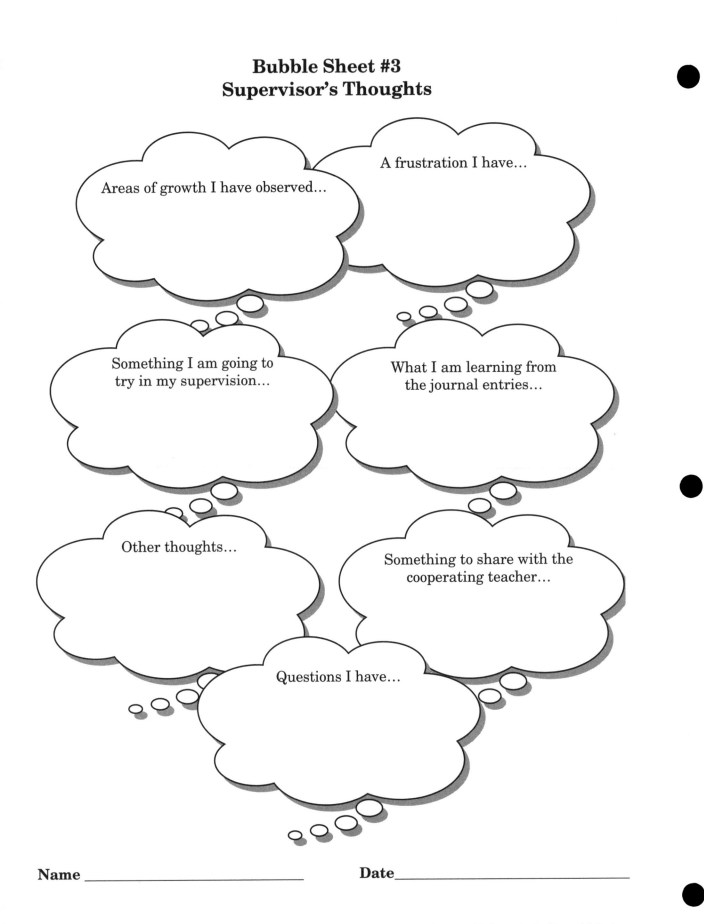

Areas of growth I have observed...

A frustration I have...

Something I am going to try in my supervision...

What I am learning from the journal entries...

Other thoughts...

Something to share with the cooperating teacher...

Questions I have...

Name _____   Date_____

ACT
Process 3.16 Problems to Possibilities—Collaborative Problem Solving

List three things related to teaching and learning that are working for you:

1. _____

2. _____

3. _____

Many common problems arise during student teaching, such as managing the classroom and discipline, feeling stress to perform as an experienced teacher when you are just a beginner, feeling pressure to complete all requirements, having concerns and self-doubts about a successful experience, taking risks in teaching and lesson planning, working with a teacher who has a different teaching philosophy, managing your time to complete all tasks, communicating your needs to your supervisor and cooperating teacher, dealing with students who display inappropriate behavior when the cooperating teacher leaves the room, and being observed while teaching.

List three problems or issues you are struggling with this semester:

1. _____

2. _____

3. _____

SELECT ONE PROBLEM

Brainstorm with your cooperating teacher, supervisor, partner, or small support group to get possible solutions to this problem. Remember to *think* in terms of *observable* teaching behaviors.

Problem	Possibilities
	1.
	2.
	3.
	4.
	5.
	6.

PARTNERS

Support from other student teachers is important while you are completing your practicum. One way to work together is to find a partner in your school who is also student teaching. He or she may be from the same college or a different one.

Observe each other teach and share your ideas.

Share your lesson plans and offer suggestions.

Share materials and resources from your education library.

Talk to each other about the joys and frustrations of being a beginning teacher.

INFORMAL SMALL GROUPS

Create a small informal group that can meet regularly during the semester. You could select a biweekly topic to discuss that relates to a common student teaching issue such as classroom management, or each session could be "open" for topics that arise. Hold your meetings at the school site or back at the college. If you host meetings at your school, rotate the classroom and have each student teacher share the materials and lessons in her or his room before you begin the discussion. You can learn a lot just by visiting other people's classrooms.

Whose classroom would you like to visit?

FORMAL MEETINGS WITH SUPERVISOR

Your supervisor may want to set up a meeting with all the students she is supervising this semester. This is an opportunity for "critical conversations" about the issues that affect you while you are student teaching. What do student teachers want to talk about? What are your issues for critical conversations?

These models can provide more support and peer supervision in addition to gaining more feedback about your teaching.

ACT
Process 3.18 Connecting the Cooperating
Teacher to the College

A major part of supervision is building trust and relationships with the people who are supervising. The more the cooperating teacher and other important people at the site know about your college program, the better understanding they will have about your professional preparation.

WAYS TO INCLUDE THE COOPERATING TEACHER

- Invite the cooperating teacher, principal, and department chair to events on campus.
- Assist in providing a library card to your cooperating teacher to use materials from your college.
- Share your cooperating teacher's name with college professors who may want to ask him to be a guest speaker.
- Encourage your cooperating teacher to attend any orientation meetings on campus provided by the Practicum Experiences Office.
- Hand deliver all materials to your cooperating teacher that will assist in your supervision.
- Encourage the cooperating teacher to attend the thank-you reception.
- Other

What other ways can you think of to bridge the gap between the college and school?

Ask your cooperating teacher what he would see as a supportive measure to assisting him in being a good supervisor.

If your teacher preparation program offers courses or workshops, invite your teacher to attend.

REFLECT

Three ways you may use to reflect on your practice during student teaching are listed on this page. Select the methods of reflection that will stimulate your thinking. Write in an *Inquiry Journal* during student teaching. This writing will serve as a data source for solving problems over time. Uncover your own assumptions, biases, and dispositions as you write in your journal several times each week.

✓ **Inquiry: Teacher Research as a Tool for Solving Classroom Problems and Enhancing Student Learning**

What is the nature of student interaction in this school and the classrooms you have observed? Is there anything that is making you uncomfortable? Write about it.

_____

_____

_____

Review the *Key Questions* in the PLAN section of this chapter. Which questions are still confusing? List them below and set up a time to discuss them with your cooperating teacher or supervisor.

_____

_____

_____

✓ **Self-Reflection: Analyze Your Teaching Strategies to Enhance Student Learning** (Use the processes in Chapter 3 to guide your self-reflection.)

Which reflective tools will you use?_____

_____

How will you use self-reflection to guide your student teaching progress?

_____

_____

✓ **Critique: Feedback from Your Supervisor and Cooperating Teacher to Guide Your Planning, Instructional Practice, and Professionalism**

How will your supervisor and cooperating teacher give you feedback? Will your cooperating teacher use the feedback form in this text? How will you schedule "quality conversations"?

_____

_____

_____

Chapter 4

Classroom Management: Organizing Time and Space for Effective Teaching and Learning

How Do I Create a Positive Learning Environment for All Students?

Learn not to take yourself so seriously. Take the experience seriously, but learn to laugh at yourself and your mistakes. Enter the classroom with a sense of humor and humility. If it weren't for mistakes, we wouldn't learn. There are lots of ups and downs in the practicum. This is your opportunity to make risk-free mistakes. So, take risks!

Student Teacher

A teacher is only as good as the learning environment he can create. How many times have you been part of a classroom where you knew the teacher was brilliant, but he just couldn't engage the learners or create an interesting lesson? We have all been in that situation. Creating a positive classroom environment and being able to design curriculum through effective lesson plans is the foundation for student learning.

Setting up a classroom and establishing routines are key components of classroom management. If your cooperating teacher does not have a permanent classroom, discuss how she adapts to this situation. Your cooperating teacher has already made decisions about how her classroom will be organized. Continue to observe the ways in which she has established procedures and how she follows up with her students. If you are student teaching in the fall, you will be able to observe how your cooperating teacher actually introduces and maintains the routines in her classroom. Try to visit the school before the fall session begins and assist the teacher in organizing her physical space. Ask her why she puts things in certain places and why she has created this organization. Is she trying anything new this year? Which procedures or systems is she retaining from previous years? Remember you are a guest in this classroom and you will be following the routines and procedures this classroom teacher has already established. You may observe things you do not agree with or that you would do differently in your classroom. Try to learn and understand why the teacher would do it this way. Use these differences of perspective as opportunities for your own journal writing and reflection.

This chapter on classroom management includes activities related to organizing the physical space, establishing classroom routines, setting boundaries for acceptable behavior, learning about students, and engaging students in learning. Each of these topics contributes to the overall "classroom climate" the teacher is creating as part of her management system.

Classroom management is often associated with classroom discipline or class control. Gaining and maintaining student attention throughout the lesson or creating a respectful environment would be a more appropriate way to think about your classroom setting. Years ago, an effective teacher may have been one that kept his class orderly and had complete classroom control. Today, you of course want a sense of order and routine, but the goal for a student teacher is to engage the learners, to have them understand the material, concept, or idea being presented.

The design of effective classroom management strategies and the incorporation of them in daily planning are the best techniques for preventing disruption and discipline problems. An effective teacher does recognize the fact that sometimes no matter what you do there will be a difficult student or situation that needs to be addressed. This issue will be discussed in a later chapter.

Your disposition and attitude as a teacher are critical factors in designing a well-organized classroom conducive to learning. If you do not have the respect of the students and if you cannot gain and maintain their attention, you will not be able to teach your lessons. Respect comes from giving respect and providing an atmosphere of respect for others. Do you smile? Do you greet students pleasantly at the door? Are you organized? Do you like to talk with students one on one? Do you move around the room? Would you consider yourself a positive force in the classroom? Do you respect differences and promote fairness for all?

Classroom management is typically the most challenging aspect of student teaching. Successful management minimizes discipline problems and leads to more effective teaching and learning. Use your CONNECT page as a resource to learning more about effective management by reading, talking with other experienced teachers, and using the Internet to connect to successful strategies. Observe as many teachers' classrooms as possible and ask them how they organize and maintain routines in their classrooms. A respectful environment that is organized and maintained will provide more time for teaching and learning.

Discussing Professional Standards

QUALITY CONVERSATIONS TO ENHANCE STUDENT LEARNING

National standards guide new teacher preparation in the United States. The INTASC created 10 principles for effective teaching. These principles are offered to you as a way to focus your attention on these key elements of practice. The "bottom line" is all about student learning. Are your students learning? How do you know?

Use these pages in each chapter to frame a quality conversation with your cooperating teacher and university supervisor. Don't be afraid to ask your own questions, too. Also use the REFLECT pages at the end of each chapter to deepen your thinking and to continue your quality conversations throughout the practium experience and into your first year of teaching.

INTASC Principles

Focus for Chapter 4

Discuss:

Principle #2   The teacher understands how children learn and develop, and can provide learning opportunities that support their intellectual, social, and personal development.

Principle #5   The teacher uses an understanding of individual and group motivation and behavior to create a learning environment that encourages positive social interaction, active engagement in learning, and self-motivation.

ASK YOURSELF   What do these principles mean to me right now? How will I know if I have achieved these principles?

DISCUSS WITH YOUR SUPERVISOR OR COOPERATING TEACHER

How will your supervisor/cooperating teacher know if you have achieved these principles? What evidence will you have to demonstrate these skills to them?

How will you know if your students have learned as a result of your teaching?

PLAN

USE ADVICE FROM FORMER STUDENT TEACHERS

Talk to student teachers who have just completed the experience and review the tips below to guide you.

- Plan a routine that works for both you and your cooperating teacher and try to be consistent throughout the semester. Your students will respond to you as a teacher if they see you working together.
- Be a "presence" in the classroom for the students—even when you are not teaching!
- Visit other classrooms to observe how teachers organize their space and set up their routines.

PROCESS YOUR EXPERIENCE

Respond to the Key Questions below by completing the process pages in each chapter. These ACTs will encourage you to deepen your thinking about teaching and learning. Write on the pages and save them to review at the end of the experience.

KEY QUESTIONS

1. How do I organize classroom space for effective teaching?

2. What is a classroom profile?

3. How do I construct and use a sociogram?

4. What are the purposes of classroom routines?

5. How are rules, rewards, and consequences part of classroom management?

6. How do I gain and maintain student attention during teaching time?

7. How can I use time effectively?

8. How can I create a community of learners in my classroom?

PLAN

TAKE CARE OF YOURSELF AND AVOID STRESS

Plan to avoid the typical stresses of student teaching by following advice from cooperating teachers and university supervisors.

PLAN FREE TIME!

Part of taking care of yourself means not giving up all the fun things in your life while you are student teaching. Do you have any hobbies? Do you play any sports? What do you enjoy doing in your free time? Students in your classroom would love to hear about what you do when you are not being a teacher—it adds a human dimension to your professional role. Always be mindful of the cognitive and developmental level of your students. Be aware of personal boundaries. Keep up with a hobby and share it with your students. Perhaps you could design a lesson in which students could share what they like to do as well.

Which hobbies would you share with your students?

Would this be a good lesson to organize for them? How would you do it?

PLAN YOUR WEEK

Priority List

Done	Tasks	Priority	Complete by When?

Place things to do on the day you would like to do them.

Monday Date:	Tuesday Date:	Wednesday Date:	Thursday Date:	Friday Date:

CONNECT

CONNECT is a resource page with ideas and suggestions to support you during student teaching. Select and complete any CONNECT items that will enhance your experience in the classroom.

CONNECT with people

- Teachers at your grade level
  Talk with as many teachers as you can and visit their classrooms. Observe how they organize their materials and display their students' work. Take notes!

CONNECT with readings & resources

- Teacher education course materials
  Review all materials you read about classroom management. Star any ideas you would like to implement in your classroom this semester.
- Books and authors to explore on the Internet or at your local library
  Quantum Teaching: Orchestrating Student Success by DePorter et al. (Allyn and Bacon)
  Classroom Management for Elementary Teachers and Classroom Management for Secondary Teachers by Evertson et al. (Allyn and Bacon)
  Managing Secondary Classrooms: Strategies by Williams et al. (Allyn and Bacon)
  The Skillful Teacher by Saphier and Gower (Research for Better Teaching, Carlisle, MA)
  The Power of Their Ideas by Meier (Beacon Press)
  Teaching or Turmoil by Brierly
  101 Ways to Develop Student Self-Esteem by Canfield and Siccone (Allyn and Bacon)
  150 Ways to Increase Intrinsic Motivation in the Classroom by Raffini (Allyn and Bacon)

CONNECT technology to teaching

- Check out this website for more information about management:
  The New Teacher Page = http://www.geocities.com/athensdelphi/786z/index.htm

  Who is running your classroom? You or the students? Research shows that how a teacher manages a classroom, not disciplines students, is the most important factor influencing student learning.

ACT
Process 4.1 Who Are My Students?
Creating a Classroom Profile

With your cooperating teacher's assistance, create a profile of the students in your classroom. If you are teaching secondary or middle school, select one of your classes to review. Find the information about the students through observation, their class record, a written survey, interviews, a class questionnaire, and talking with the cooperating teacher. The more you know about the class, the easier it is to create and maintain a positive learning environment.

List the names of the students and complete the table (on the next page) by writing one or two descriptive words for each category. When complete, you will have a summary of the class you will be working with this semester. Feel free to replace these categories with those you would find more useful.

- What do you know about the students in your clasroom?

- What do you need to know about them to be an effective teacher?

- Look at the patterns on the table when you have completed it. How will you use this information to differentiate instruction?

Students' Names	Gender	Culture	Age	Language	Musical Ability	Artistic Ability	Athletic Ability	Learning Style	Learning Need

After completing the chart, review the data and think about the ways your students can contribute to the creation of a positive learning environment in your classroom.

ACT
Process 4.2A   Organizing the Physical Space
What Works?

Draw a picture of the classroom or one of the rooms you are working in this year. Include the teacher's desk, your desk, the students' desks, file cabinet, bookcases, overhead projector, computer, supply cabinet, plants, learning centers, bulletin boards, and so on.

Why do you think the teacher's desk is placed where it is?

How are student desks organized? Can all students see the teacher? Do they need to? Are they always set up this way? Does the room organization ever vary? Why?

Take a colored marker and draw the main traffic flow in the room. Is it smooth? Access to exits? Are there any obstacles?

To gain insight, ask your cooperating teacher why and for how long she has organized the space this way.

ACT
Process 4.2B Organizing the Physical Space
How Do Other Teachers Organize Their Space?

Interview your cooperating teacher and answer the questions below. Complete the chart for the level at which you are teaching. If there are several teachers at the same grade level in your school, observe informally to see whether they follow the same guiding principles for organizing the physical environment of their classrooms. Why might it be different? You may want to extend this activity to see how space arrangements may vary from grade level by interviewing other teachers and filling in the rest of this chart. Note that one teacher's response cannot be generalized to say that all middle school teachers would do it this way.

	Early Childhood	*Elementary*	*Middle School*	*High School*
Student Desks How are they organized? Why?				
Teacher's Desk Where is it placed? Why?				
Bulletin Boards or Learning Centers How are they used? Why?				
Supplies and Materials Where are they located? Who gets to use them? Why?				
Computer(s) Where are they? How are they used? Why?				
Other?				

ACT
Process 4.3   Constructing a Sociogram

One way to illustrate the dynamics in a classroom is to construct a sociogram. Do this with your cooperating teacher to gain insights into the work preferences of the students. You can use the information to design cooperative groups or teams. It will also let you know what the students think of each other and where you may have to step in to include some students that you may not have realized were excluded.

Step 1. Ask students in the classroom to list three students, by first, second, and third choice, whom they would prefer to work with in the classroom. (Make a distinction between work partners and social partners outside of school.) Tell them it is for possible future group projects and that you may use it to try to create teams with at least one person with whom they prefer to work.

Step 2. Have the students write why they selected each student. This will give you some insight, and themes may repeat themselves.

Step 3. Collect the data and make a grid with students' names across the top and down the left side. Graph paper works well. Place a 1, 2, or 3 under each student's name as indicated to show choices.

SAMPLE

	José	*Michael*	*Julia*	*Laura*
José	—	1	3	2
Michael	3	—	1	2
Julia	3	2	—	1
Laura	3	2	1	—

Step 4. Tally choices to indicate most preferred working partners (commonly called *stars*) and least selected working partners (referred to as *isolates*).

Step 5. Use a square for males and a triangle for females and cut the shapes to represent each student in your class. Place on a poster board to illustrate how students made choices. Draw arrows with choice number pointed to student. Using three colors for 1, 2, and 3 works well. The visual display will illustrate stars and isolates.

(Note: THIS IS A CONFIDENTIAL PROCESS. DO NOT SHARE WITH STUDENTS.)

SAMPLE OF FIRST CHOICES

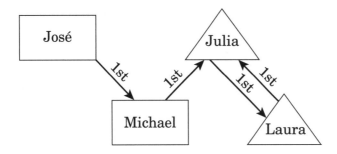

USING THE SOCIOGRAM TO LEARN ABOUT YOUR CLASSROOM

This is a good exercise for the cooperating teacher and student teacher to do together.

1. Read the choices and reasons why students selected preferred working partners. Were there any surprises? Were there common themes for selecting students? What else did you notice?

2. Review the data on the grid and write your initial impressions of how it describes the classroom relationships. Discuss and compare to your cooperating teacher's impressions. What do you notice?

3. Build the sociogram using triangles and squares. After the symbols have been placed on poster board, glue and draw arrows indicating preferences. What do you see?

ACT
Process 4.4   Establishing Routines and Why They Are Important

Routines are important for maintaining consistency and moving through a teaching day in a manner that students can expect. Routines can save valuable time and energy that can be put into academic areas. They can also be used to teach respect, to model expected behaviors, and to generally promote the positive attitude and environment you are seeking to create in the classroom.

Observe your classroom for routines that have been established or that are being currently integrated into the teacher's day.

As you observe or discuss routines with your cooperating teacher, think about the following:

1. What is the purpose of the routine?
2. Are the students familiar with this routine? How do you know?
3. How does your cooperating teacher reinforce a routine already established?
4. How does your cooperating teacher present a new routine to the class?
5. What other skill(s) are students learning while participating in this routine?
6. Are routines saving time that can be used for teaching?

ROUTINE CATEGORIES AND EXAMPLES

1. Examples of **Opening Routines**
   - Attendance and how to get work/assignments to students who are absent
   - Lunch count if applicable
   - Collecting homework and recording it

2. Examples of **Operating Procedures**
   - Walking to classes or passing in the halls
   - Leaving during class time
   - Fire drills

3. Examples of **Teaching Routines**
   - Expected behavior in classroom
   - Class discussion procedures for listening to others
   - Noise level for group work
   - Students who forgot books or materials
   - Activities for students who finish early
   - Who is responsible for materials

4. Examples of **Closing Routines**
   - Collecting work
   - Leaving classroom
   - Cleaning up

List other routines you observed:

What have you learned about routines and their affect on the classroom learning environment?

Rules, rewards, and consequences are part of a teacher's management system. Because they vary significantly by grade and age of students, you as a student teacher must understand and observe them. Complete the chart for the grade level in which you are teaching. Interview other student teachers or classroom teachers to get a sense of what is appropriate for other grade levels. Teachers who include the establishment of fair rules and consequences as part of the respectful learning environment generally have fewer discipline issues and disruptions during teaching time. The key is "fairness" and equal, respectful treatment for all students.

Ask your cooperating teacher how the rules, rewards, and consequences were established. Did students have any input in creating them? How long has he been using this system? What other systems has he used in the past? Why did he change? The key to rules, rewards, and consequences is communicating them to the students BEFORE they break them.

Complete the chart for your grade level. How effectively would your rules, rewards, and consequences transfer to other grade levels?

	Early Childhood	*Elementary*	*Middle School*	*High School*
Rules What are they? Who created them? Are they visibly displayed?				
Rewards What are they? Material items? Verbal praise? No homework? When are rewards given? Do they work? Do they match the rules?				
Consequences What are they? How often are they used? Do they fit the misbehavior? Are they grade-level appropriate?				

What is your impression of these rules, rewards, and consequences? Would you use any of these in your own classroom? Why? Why not?

ACT
Process 4.5B   Student Conferences and Contacts

A short conference with a student individually or in a small group can make a difference in the ways students respond in class. Instead of speaking directly out loud to a student in front of his peers, ask the student to see you after class.

Create a conference report so you can note that this is an official meeting and that the student is on notice for a specific reason.

SAMPLE

Conference Report

Student's Name: _____ **Date:** _____

Reason for Conference:

_____

_____

_____

_____

Summary of Conference:_____

_____

_____

_____

_____

Follow-up and Goal:_____

_____

_____

Signature of Teacher _____

Signature of Student_____

Student Contract

Student's Name:_____

I state that I will *(change a certain behavior)*_____

_____. I will measure my success by *(how the behavior*

will be noted as being done) ._____

_____

_____

_____

For successful demonstration *(I will receive a reward; list reward [see page 97])*.

_____

_____

_____

_____

Signed (teacher):_____   **Date:**

Signed (student):_____   **Date:**

The contract can also be designed for groups by changing *I* to *we*.

Create your own contracts to prevent problems!

ACT
Process 4.5C   Rewards

Rewards are the best part of rules and consequences. Rewards can be offered to individual students or to the whole class. The key here is to have the students recognize the reward as something that is valuable to them and worth working for.

Ask your students what they would consider a "reward" and integrate it into your classroom management system.

Your students' ideas for rewards:

_____

_____

Compare their ideas with a typical list generated by elementary and high school students:

SAMPLES

ELEMENTARY REWARDS	*SECONDARY REWARDS*
Free time	Free time
Watch a video	Read a magazine
Do errands for the teacher	Work on computer
Lead the line	See a film/video
Go to the reading center	Food
Pick out a book	Class trip
Play with the pet in class	Play sports during day
Listen to music in class	Listen to CD in class
Stickers	Use the video camera
Pencils	Be coach's assistant
Ice cream	Make a T-shirt
A certificate	Teach a class
Pizza party	Free homework pass
Magic markers	Read a newspaper
Free recess	
Sit next to a friend for a day	

ACT
Process 4.6   Gaining and Maintaining Student Attention

Teachers need to have students' attention at various times during the day to give instructions, to move the class to another room, to make announcements, and so forth. Observe how your cooperating teacher gains and maintains attention for these noninstructional activities. Often, these are integrated into the daily routine and instructional class time. It is important to streamline these activities or a valuable class period can be lost attending to tasks unrelated to the curriculum. Here are some questions to guide your observation and learning.

STARTING THE CLASS PERIOD OR SCHOOL DAY/BEGINNING THE LESSON

Integrating noninstructional announcements, collecting homework, and opening exercises often take place at the beginning of the school day or class period. How does your teacher do this? How is it included in the time allotted for the lesson?

How does your cooperating teacher initially gain students' attention to shift from noninstructional announcements to instructional curriculum? Does she use a story? A prop? A question? Does she connect what is coming up in the lesson to the students' own experiences?

List any ways the teacher motivates and gains attention:

_____

_____

THE LESSON

How does your cooperating teacher maintain this attention if there is a whole class? If there are small groups, is it different? How does she ensure all students are engaged in a learning experience? Does she walk around? How does she interact with students to keep them on task? Does she call on students?

List any maintaining management strategies you observed.

_____

CLOSING THE LESSON AND ENDING THE CLASS PERIOD: WHAT'S THE DIFFERENCE?

How does your cooperating teacher complete the lesson? How does she know the students learned? How does she check for understanding? Are there noninstructional directions that need to be given at the end of class? Is there time for questions and answers, or does the lesson just end? Is there time for students to do homework? How does the teacher close the lesson and end the class period? How are these things different?

List the management techniques for closing you observed:

How does opening, maintaining, and closing a lesson in a predictable and organized way contribute to student learning?

_____

ACT
Process 4.7 Creating a Community of Learners

Discuss the following approaches to team building with your cooperating teacher. Check the line as you discuss each method.

_____ 1. **Sharing time.** Students come to school with a lot on their minds. If it is appropriate, allow for a short period of time every day to let students listen to one another. Use this as an opportunity to have students be good listeners and speakers. Plus, the conversation is real life!

_____ 2. **Partners.** At all grade levels, students are absent or miss parts of a school day. Assigning partners encourages students to care about each other and take responsibility for the academic material. In secondary school, a log may be more appropriate than partners. This lists homework assignments and other information important to the class. Absent students read it the day they come in and can talk to the log writer.

_____ 3. **Teams.** Within the elementary classroom, create small learning teams for various activities or projects. Let the teams create names, slogans, and strategies for completing assignments. Rotate teams often so the individuals in the class as a whole have many opportunities to work with different students. You may want to create the teams yourself at first to make sure all students are included and that team making doesn't become a popularity contest. One strategy for knowing your classroom and making teams is using the sociogram technique.

_____ 4. **Groups.** Within the secondary classroom, create either cooperative or collaborative groups to encourage team building while achieving the goal of the lesson. Give each student an assigned role.

_____ 5. **Compliments.** At the end of the day or a class period, have students recognize one another through compliments. You or your cooperating teacher may need to model appropriate compliments before students know how to do it. A student who receives a compliment must acknowledge it by saying thank you.

_____ 6. **List your ideas:** _____

_____

How do these ideas create a positive learning environment?

You may have experience being a new student in school. Perhaps you know what it feels like to enter a classroom that has already been established. The students know each other, the rules have been established, and friends have already been made. If you have never been a new student, think about how this student must feel. It doesn't matter how old the student is, whether he is in preschool or high school, there are always nervous feelings when someone enters a new environment in the middle of a year.

When students move after a school year has started, there are often transition issues. Sometimes the move is because of problems in the family, and other times there may be celebration of success (e.g., a job promotion created the move). In either case, students have adjustments to make.

HOW TO EASE A STUDENT INTO YOUR CLASS/CLASSROOM

- Introduce the student to the class and highlight some positive aspects you notice.

- Interview the student privately to find out why she moved, what curriculum she was using in the previous school, and so on. Ask the student what she likes about school, what she is most nervous about, and similar questions

- Connect with the secretary in the school office or with your cooperating teacher to get any school records from the previous school.

- Connect the student to one or two students in your classroom (you might have designated "Welcome to Our Class" students) who are trained to do this and who *want* to do this! They can give a tour of the school, eat lunch with the student, walk him around the high school, or play with him on the playground.

- Carefully integrate the student into groups and lessons, observing reading level and ability to complete tasks independently.

- Talk with the parents as soon as possible to learn more about the student.

- Present the new student with a "Welcome Wagon" gift (have these all prepared for any new students who enter during the year). Include new pencils, paper, stickers, or high school notebooks—things related to the grade level that will get the student on board quickly. Consider asking town sponsors to pay for these Welcome Wagon gifts as a way to advertise the town.

ACT
Process 4.9   Routines Create Class Learning Time

A major purpose of establishing routines is to save time that can be used to teach. Analyze the routines that already exist in your classroom to see how much time is spent on routine activities.

Compare this to your lesson plans and how much time you include in lessons that relate to routines. Sometimes student teachers don't even write down time for routines and then run short on the core of the lesson because setting up the lesson took so long!

Complete the time for the routines listed and add some of your own. Record how much time you spend during one class period. Calculate how much time you might spend daily, weekly, and monthly just on collecting papers! Are you completing routine tasks as efficiently as possible?

Routines	Lesson Time Spent	Daily Time Spent	Weekly Time Spent	Monthly Time Spent
Passing out papers				
Collecting papers				
Recording homework				
Taking attendance				
Textbook distribution				

Ask your cooperating teacher to assist you in looking at how you spend time on routines and how this relates to good lesson planning and creating a positive learning environment for all students.

Remember, the goal is not just to save time for time itself, but to take that time and turn it into valuable learning opportunities for students. Routines and procedures should allow for flexible time and unscheduled events. Fire drills, students coming in from other classes to share information, the principal dropping by to visit and talk with students, and so on, are all part of a typical school day. Don't get frustrated by interruptions and changes in routines. A teacher is never fully in control of time. Learn to go with the flow and live for the teachable moment. Establish routines and be prepared to change them if there is an opportunity for learning.

ACT
Process 4.10A   Things to Do—Daily Reminders

Date: _____   **Check When Completed:**_____

____   1. _____

____   2. _____

____   3. _____

____   4. _____

____   5. _____

____   6. _____

____   7. _____

____   8. _____

____   9. _____

____   10. _____

____   11. _____

____   12. _____

NOTES

ACT
Process 4.10B   Planning Calendar

	Classes You Are Teaching	*Course Requirements*	*Student Teaching Requirements*
Week Date			
Week Date			
Week Date			
Week Date			
Week Date			

REFLECT

Three ways you may use to reflect on your practice during student teaching are listed on this page. Select the methods of reflection that will stimulate your thinking. Write in an *Inquiry Journal* during student teaching. This writing will serve as a data source for solving problems over time. Uncover your own assumptions, biases, and dispositions as you write in your journal several times each week.

✓ **Inquiry: Teacher Research as a Tool for Solving Classroom Problems and Enhancing Student Learning**

What emotions do you see or hear as you enter this classroom (or observe different classes that enter the same room)—for example, enthusiasm, anger, happiness, passiveness, and so on? Why do you think these emotions are present?

_____

_____

_____

Review the *Key Questions* in the PLAN section of this chapter. Which questions are still confusing? List them below and set up a time to discuss them with your cooperating teacher or supervisor.

_____

_____

_____

✓ **Self-Reflection: Analyze Your Teaching Strategies to Enhance Student Learning** (Use the processes in Chapter 3 to guide your self-reflection.)

How do the students interact when the teacher isn't looking? Do you think this will happen when you are teaching? Why? Why not?

_____

_____

_____

✓ **Critique: Feedback from Your Supervisor and Cooperating Teacher to Guide Your Planning, Instructional Practice, and Professionalism**

What suggestions, ideas, or comments have your supervisor/cooperating teacher given you in regard to classroom and time management? Where are you collecting these suggestions so you can refer to them later?

_____

_____

_____

_____

Chapter 5

Behavior Management and Discipline Strategies

How Do I Respond to Uncooperative Students?

Try not to get discouraged. You are a new teacher, not a seasoned professional. Do your best with students who misbehave, and don't beat yourself up about any situation. There are some days when your students will be angels. On other days you will think they were sent to punish you for past wrongs. Always try your best and continue to learn.

Student Teacher

In theory, if a teacher organizes an effective classroom, designs lessons that meet the needs of the students, and presents information in engaging ways, she should not have problems with uncooperative students. In practice, however, all teachers encounter cases in which students break the rules and they must face consequences. In the classroom management chapter (Chapter 4), the concepts of rules, rewards, and consequences were introduced as a means of organizing an effective learning environment. This chapter relates to whether the students respond to the management system created and how students who are not cooperative can be helped.

There are varying degrees of infractions that you as a student teacher need to observe and be aware of as you move into the role of teacher. A student sleeping in the back of the classroom is certainly not on task, but sleeping is a very different violation from a student who hits another student in class. Both require intervention and consequences, but the reaction from you as the teacher may be quite different. More serious violent actions from students should always be reported to your cooperating teacher so the school policies can be followed. Discuss with your cooperating teacher how different kinds of rule breaking require different responses.

Repeated offenses by the same student also may require a different response from you when you are in the role of teacher. A student who forgets her homework for the first time should not be disciplined the same way as the student who has forgotten several times. One definition of discipline is "to train or develop by instruction and exercise, especially in self-control." As the teacher, you can use these infractions of the rules as opportunities to teach self-responsibility.

Classroom management and discipline continue to be the two areas in which student teachers request more information and preparation. Often, student teachers express frustration in taking over a class from their cooperating teachers, because they see that the teacher doesn't have any problems and then the students misbehave for them. One reason for this is that your cooperating teacher has a command of the class and the students "know" they can't get away with bad behavior. Experienced teachers know their students and can eliminate problems by "the look" or by subtle body language or movement toward a potential problem. When a student teacher "takes over" a class, the students often "test" the student teacher. In an effort to "be a friend" to the class, the student teacher loses control and the students misbehave. One lesson for student teachers is to be *friendly* but *not a friend* to the students.

In all cases of discipline, the cooperating teacher needs to be consulted, especially if parents need to be called or notes written home about a student's misbehavior or lack of attention to schoolwork. This is your cooperating teacher's classroom, and all discipline strategies must be implemented with his consent.

For the small number of issues that do arise, use the processes in this chapter to guide you as you strive to create a positive learning environment.

Discussing Professional Standards

QUALITY CONVERSATIONS TO ENHANCE STUDENT LEARNING

National standards guide new teacher preparation in the United States. The INTASC created 10 principles for effective teaching. These principles are offered to you as a way to focus your attention on these key elements of practice. The "bottom line" is all about student learning. Are your students learning? How do you know?

Use these pages in each chapter to frame a quality conversation with your cooperating teacher and university supervisor. Don't be afraid to ask your own questions, too. Also use the REFLECT pages at the end of each chapter to deepen your thinking and to continue your quality conversations throughout the practium experience and into your first year of teaching.

INTASC Principles

Focus for Chapter 5

Discuss:

Principle #6   The teacher uses knowledge of effective verbal, nonverbal, and media communication techniques to foster active inquiry, collaboration, and supportive interaction in the classroom.

Review:

Principle #2   The teacher understands how children learn and develop, and can provide learning opportunities that support their intellectual, social, and personal development.

Principle #5   The teacher uses an understanding of individual and group motivation and behavior to create a learning environment that encourages positive social interaction, active engagement in learning, and self-motivation.

ASK YOURSELF   What do these principles mean to me right now? How will I know if I have achieved these principles?

DISCUSS WITH YOUR SUPERVISOR OR COOPERATING TEACHER

How will your supervisor/cooperating teacher know if you have achieved these principles? What evidence will you have to demonstrate these skills to them?

How will you know if your students have learned as a result of your teaching?

PLAN

USE ADVICE FROM FORMER STUDENT TEACHERS

Talk to student teachers who have just completed the experience and review the tips below to guide you.

- Be sure your students understand that you don't like the *behavior*, not them personally.
- Avoid meaningless punishments such as writing 50 sentences; instead, have the student write a paragraph or letter explaining why she should not have behaved a certain way.
- Observe students behaving and compliment them immediately!
- Be sure to model the rules you are monitoring.
- Schedule individual meetings with students rather than speaking in front of the class.

PROCESS YOUR EXPERIENCE

Respond to the Key Questions below by completing the process pages in each chapter. These ACTs will encourage you to deepen your thinking about teaching and learning. Write on the pages and save them to review at the end of the experience.

KEY QUESTIONS

1. What is my cooperating teacher's and school's philosophy of discipline?

2. What should I think about before disciplining a student?

3. What types of common student discipline issues should I expect?

4. What are some problem-solving strategies I can use?

5. How do I know if it is a more serious issue and what do I do?

6. How can I avoid discipline problems?

PLAN

TAKE CARE OF YOURSELF AND AVOID STRESS

Plan to avoid the typical stresses of student teaching by following advice from cooperating teachers and university supervisors.

SHARE YOUR CLASSROOM!

Invite someone to visit your classroom so you can "show off" for a day (or morning or class period)! Show and tell your visitor about all the work you have done this semester. Don't dwell on any negative issues or discipline problems you have been trying to solve, don't ask for help, and don't seek advice. Simply make this a showcase of all your proudest moments!

Who could you invite?

PLAN YOUR WEEK

Priority List

Done	Tasks	Priority	Complete by When?

Place things to do on the day you would like to do them.

Monday Date:	Tuesday Date:	Wednesday Date:	Thursday Date:	Friday Date:

CONNECT

CONNECT is a resource page with ideas and suggestions to support you during student teaching. Select and complete any CONNECT items that will enhance your experience in the classroom.

CONNECT *with people*

- Cooperating teacher(s)
  Talk with your cooperating teacher to learn about students who are "at risk" in your classroom.
- Guidance counselor, school nurse, school psychologist
  Learn as much as you can about the support systems available to students

---

CONNECT *with readings & resources*

- Books and authors to explore on the Internet or at your local library
  Changing Attitudes: A Strategy for Motivating Students to Learn and Thinking Critically about Attitudes by Ruggiero (Allyn and Bacon)
  Discipline with Dignity by Corwin and Mendler (ASCD)
  Solving Discipline Problems and The *Three Faces of Discipline for the Elementary Teacher* by Wolfgang (Allyn and Bacon)
  School Discipline and School Violence by Hyman et al. (Allyn and Bacon)
  A Guide to Positive Discipline by Keating et al. (Allyn and Bacon)
  The Student Teacher's Guide: Intervention Strategies for the Most Common Behavior Problems Encountered by Student Teachers by McCarney (Hawthorne)
  Classroom Management—A Case Study Handbook for Teachers of Challenging Learners by Osborne and DiMattia (Carolina Academic Press)

CONNECT *technology to teaching*

- Seek out chat sites
  Talk to other student teachers or beginning teachers about your issues and try to create solutions to your discipline problems
- Find 10 ways to help kids who have trouble paying attention
  Check out NEA's On-line News for ways to keep students in focus at
  http://www.nea.org/neatoday/
- A little bit of everything = http://www.theteachernetwork.com and
  http://www.learningpage.com

ACT
Process 5.1   School Policies for Disruptive Students

1. What is the school's discipline policy? Is it written? Posted for students to see? Get a copy and review it with your cooperating teacher. Do you understand all parts of the policy?

   Is it clear to you when it is appropriate to send a student out of the classroom to the principal's office?

   List three key points of the school's discipline procedure:

   _____

   _____

   _____

2. What is your cooperating teacher's philosophy and policy? Ask him to share any specific rules and procedures with you. Do the students understand the rules and follow them? What happens when they don't? Review ACT Process 4.5 from Chapter 4.

   List three key points about your cooperating teacher's classroom philosophy here:

   _____

   _____

   _____

3. What is your discipline philosophy? How does it compare to the school and classroom where you are currently student teaching? Describe an incident that has occurred and show how it could be handled two different ways depending on the teacher's philosophy.

   Incident: _____

   _____

   _____

   _____

   One way to respond: _____

   _____

   _____

   _____

   Another way to respond: _____

   _____

   _____

   _____

ACT
Process 5.2A Common Classroom Misbehaviors
What Can I Expect?

Classroom disruption and behavior issues are unfortunately part of the school day. Common classroom misbehaviors need to be anticipated and expected. Plan your general responses to each of these behaviors. Be consistent with all students. These responses are part of your classroom management system in the previous chapter.

Common problems vary in early childhood, elementary, middle school, and high school settings. Approaches to dealing with common problems also vary. How do you know the difference between a common misbehavior and one that is more serious?

A student found sleeping in the back of a classroom in a high school or early childhood setting may be seen as a common problem (for very different reasons!), but a student found sleeping in an elementary school classroom may be looked at more seriously as a sign of other issues.

Some common problems you may see in your setting are listed below. List whether the problem is common at all levels or just one. Which ones are you seeing in your school or classroom?

Common Problem	*Grade Level You Might See This Behavior*	*Is This a Problem in Your Setting? How Will You Respond When This Happens?*
Not bringing materials to class (books, pencils, etc.)		
Not completing homework		
Bringing toys to class		
Showing up late for class		
Disruptive talk during lessons		
Throwing things (spit balls, planes, desk, etc.)		
Not showing up for detention assigned by teacher		
Sleeping in class		

Identifying common problems is important. How do teachers in your setting effectively respond to these inappropriate student behaviors? How will you respond to them?

Why is it important to be consistent with all students?

ACT
Process 5.2B Common Classroom Misbehaviors
How Often Do They Occur?

Four categories for misbehaviors are listed in the chart below with some possible steps to take to deal with each. A key to understanding discipline issues is to observe whether the problem is with one student or a classroom behavior pattern for a number of students. Ask your cooperating teacher to share other typical issues that take place in this school and possible ways to solve them for this age group. You must remain consistent with the school's procedure and offer fair solutions.

Common Problems	*What You Need to Do*
Chronic Work Avoidance Evidenced by being absent regularly, fooling around in class, not passing in assignments, tardiness, sleeping in class, etc.	• Make sure student is capable of work • Keep accurate records of what is missing • Talk with cooperating teacher • Let student know how assignments affect grade • Talk with parents • Other?
Habitual Rule Breaking Evidenced by calling out in class, not bringing pencil to class regularly, being talkative, forgetting other materials, skipping classes, etc.	• Use consequences established • Try behavior modification systems • Talk with student privately • Discuss issue with cooperating teacher • Talk with parents • Other?
Hostile Verbal Outbursts Evidenced by angry loud yelling, chip-on-the-shoulder attitude, defiance when asked to complete assignments, etc.	• Determine whether the outburst is just momentary • Don't engage in a power struggle • Remove the student if anger persists • Talk with cooperating teacher • Talk with principal • Talk with guidance counselor • Talk with parents • Other?
Fighting, Destruction, Weapons, Alcohol Abuse, Drug Abuse, Sexual Harassment, Bullying Evidenced by hallway pushing, violence with peers, threats, glazed look in class, etc.	• Send a student for help • Disperse crowds that may gather to watch • Calmly talk; do not shout or scream • Report the incident immediately • Other?

ACT
Process 5.2C Common Classroom Misbehaviors
What Are They? In the School Setting?

Observe the classroom and school. List the *three most serious* unacceptable behaviors you observe. Note how they have been handled, and how you could avoid them in the future.

Unacceptable Behavior	How Handled	How to Avoid
1.		
2.		
3.		

List three *less serious offenses.* How were they handled? How could you avoid them in the future?

Unacceptable Behavior	How Handled	How to Avoid
1.		
2.		
3.		

Discuss these issues with your cooperating teacher to determine how she would address them. Do not make any disciplining decisions without the consent of your cooperating teacher. You need to work as a team so the students see you both as teachers.

ACT
Process 5.3 Problems to Possibilities
Specific Problem Solving

WHAT WILL YOU DO IF...

You have a class clown telling jokes during your classes?

You have a bully in your classroom who hits one student every day?

You have a student who lies to you about doing her own work?

You have a student who displays passive-aggressive behavior?

As a student teacher, you will observe many problem situations in your classroom. To maintain an academic focus and a climate for learning, you also need to respond quickly to misbehavior. If you don't, it can escalate and take away from learning.

STEP ONE: SELECT A PROBLEM

Select one problem or issue that you are really having difficulty with this semester.

_____

STEP TWO: CREATE QUESTIONS

List three questions you have about this student's problem or life situation and try to get them answered.

Q1: _____
Answer:

Q2: _____
Answer:

Q3: _____
Answer:

STEP THREE: LEARN ABOUT THE STUDENT TO ANSWER THE QUESTIONS

1. Major Points from Student's School History

   Find out as much as you can about the student. Write a mini-case study that gives a fuller picture of who the student is and where she has been in school. Background information is usually available in the student's file. Ask the cooperating teacher for permission to view the file.

2. Observe the Student in Action

   Ask yourself, "What is the purpose of this behavior from the student's point of view?"

STEP FOUR: DETERMINE POSSIBILITIES

Given the behavior and the history of this student in school, determine several possible ways in which you could change this behavior pattern. Review behavior modification techniques from your strategies classes.

Possibility 1:

Possibility 2:

Possibility 3:

STEP FIVE: COMPARE YOUR POSSIBILITIES

Working in a small group with other student teachers or with your cooperating teacher and supervisor, brainstorm ideas. All student teachers can list their particular problem on a post-it paper and hang on the board. Cluster the problems using the categories in ACT Process 5.2B. What do you notice about these problems? Write possible solutions on the board beneath the problem. Compare solutions to those you already thought about. Take any new ideas!

New possibilities generated:

STEP SIX: TRY A POSSIBILITY WITH YOUR PROBLEM!

Record the result here:

Did it work? Do you need to modify it? Should you try another possibility?

ACT
Process 5.4 Things to Think about Before
Disciplining a Student

☐ Who is the student?

Does this student have a prearranged plan when disruptive (e.g., sent to guidance, principal, or resource or learning center classroom)?

Is this a first offense or is this repeated misbehavior?

Does this student have a special need that has not been addressed?

Are there other adults that need to be notified when this student is disruptive?

☐ What rule did the student break?

Is it a major offense (e.g., hitting someone or possessing a weapon)?

Is it a minor offense (e.g., chewing gum or wearing a hat)?

Is it related to academic work (e.g., not doing homework or cheating)?

Is it related to work habits (e.g., not listening in class)?

☐ What did the student specifically do or say?

☐ Is this misbehavior appropriate for the student's age?

☐ Where did the misbehavior take place?

In the classroom?

On the playground, in a hallway, in the cafeteria, en route to class?

Off school grounds but near school?

☐ Is this behavior a common occurrence?

For this student?

For others in the school?

☐ Do you have personal feelings about this student?

Have you interacted positively or negatively before this?

Do you know this student at all?

☐ What are your legal rights when dealing with disruptive students?

State and local guidelines for restraining students, searching lockers, etc.?

School policies related to alcohol, drugs, weapons?

Students with educational plans?

ACT
Process 5.5 Documentation: Collecting Data on More Serious Misbehaviors

Common misbehaviors are expected and dealt with on a daily basis by teachers through appropriate responses for all students. From time to time, a teacher will have a student that does not respond and repeats this misbehavior. It is important to document student misbehaviors in these cases with dates and descriptions. This is important data to share with parents and your cooperating teacher if needed.

Date	Time/Period	What the Student Did	How You Responded

ACT
Process 5.6   When Is It Time to Seek Additional Support?

How do you know when you need more help?

_____ When you have exhausted your possibilities
_____ When the student exhibits serious problems beyond the scope of common issues
_____ When your cooperating teacher has determined the student needs additional help
_____ When parents have indicated a need for support
_____ Other

How do you know what kind of help is available for a student?

TALK TO...

_____ Teachers of students with special needs
_____ Guidance department
_____ School psychologist/school social worker
_____ Principal
_____ Department chair
_____ School nurse or health department

What should you do?

_____ Maintain accurate records of all misbehaviors with dates of offenses
_____ Write a request for help with your cooperating teacher

How do you know you haven't failed?

_____ You have tried a number of approaches with the student and documented them
_____ Your cooperating teacher has made the decision to refer the student

ACT
Process 5.7   How to Avoid Common Classroom Misbehaviors

Review these key areas that could lead to discipline problems.

- **Classroom management.** Have you structured your classroom in an orderly way to avoid potential problems? Traffic flow? Room setup?

  What could you change to avoid any further issues?

- **Lesson planning.** Have you designed lessons that meet the needs of all students so they don't get frustrated and angry? Are the lessons challenging but doable? Do you have accommodations for grouping that avoid discipline issues?

  How can you redesign lessons to avoid future discipline problems you are experiencing?

- **Discipline—Rules, rewards, and consequences.** Are the rules clearly posted and understood? Do students "own" them or are they imposed on them? Are you consistent when you apply the consequences? Do you treat all students fairly?

  What do you need to do to be sure your rules, rewards, and consequences are working to avoid problems?

KEEP TRACK OF WHAT IS WORKING!

It is so easy to stay focused on the one misbehaving student who is gaining all the attention in your classroom. You certainly want everyone to behave and listen to you. Don't forget, you are doing many things right! List the behaviors you are observing in your classroom that are positive and list why you think they are working. What are you doing to maintain that behavior? Keep it up!

Classroom Behavior	What You Are Doing	Why Is It Working?
Class is passing in papers in an orderly way every day with their names on them!	Stopping class three minutes before the bell to allow time to pass in papers.	Consistently ask students to check their names and pass in papers.

REFLECT

Three ways you may use to reflect on your practice during student teaching are listed on this page. Select the methods of reflection that will stimulate your thinking. Write in an *Inquiry Journal* during student teaching. This writing will serve as a data source for solving problems over time. Uncover your own assumptions, biases, and dispositions as you write in your journal several times each week.

✓ **Inquiry: Teacher Research as a Tool for Solving Classroom Problems and Enhancing Student Learning**

How does the teacher(s) respond to inappropriate behavior(s) throughout the day?

What do you notice works with students? What does not work? Why?

_____

_____

_____

Review the *Key Questions* in the PLAN section of this chapter. Which questions are still confusing? List them below and set up a time to discuss them with your cooperating teacher or supervisor.

_____

_____

_____

✓ **Self-Reflection: Analyze Your Teaching Strategies to Enhance Student Learning** (Use the processes in Chapter 3 to guide your self-reflection.)

How are you responding to inappropriate student behavior in the classes you are teaching? _____

What are you struggling with? _____

_____

_____

How does your daily lesson planning relate to managing student behavior?

_____

_____

_____

✓ **Critique: Feedback from Your Supervisor and Cooperating Teacher to Guide Your Planning, Instructional Practice, and Professionalism**

What are your cooperating teacher and supervisor suggesting as good strategies for behavior management and discipline?

_____

_____

_____

Chapter 6

Daily Lesson and Unit Planning

How Does Planning Relate to Effective Teaching?

The hardest part of student teaching is the PLANNING! I hate planning. I hated it when I first started, and I hate it now. However, it is the single-most important thing (followed by organization). There were days when I did not have time to plan. Those days were awful. The anxiety that came along with the knowledge that I had not planned was stifling, and the classes were chaotic. I hated those days. . . . I hated them more than I hated planning.

Student Teacher

The ability to plan high-quality lessons that engage students in learning experiences that promote thinking and understanding is the essence of good teaching. Designing curriculum is an important task for teachers and one that is becoming increasingly more important as student performance and outcomes are used to assess success in schools. High standards and clear expectations for what students should know and be able to do is currently the focus of education. Classroom planning needs to reflect these high expectations and standards.

Teachers need excellent planning and preparation skills. Knowledge of the content area that integrates the content with other disciplines and the ability to build on students' existing knowledge and teach for understanding are expected of all new teachers. In addition, teachers need to understand who their students are by understanding the students' age group, interests, and ability levels. Planning also requires a clear articulation of the goals and objectives teachers are trying to achieve. Finally, good planning and preparation requires that teachers know what materials and resources are available and how they can be used to create a positive learning experience for all students.

Student teachers often view planning as an isolated activity related to the lesson they are teaching and their requirements for student teaching. In reality, planning is a critical component of teaching, and it connects teaching to all aspects of the school day. Good lesson planning can promote positive classroom management and lessen discipline issues. The objectives in your lesson plan should relate to the learning outcomes you expect from the students. A cycle of plan, teach, assess, and reteach becomes the model for moving through the curriculum objectives. Assessments, whether formal or informal, must relate to the plan. The ultimate goal for planning and assessment is student learning. Do your plans promote understanding and accomplishment or are they just telling students what to do?

Teachers plan in two ways: long range and short term. Yearly and quarterly planning are long-range planning skills. This is an opportunity for the teacher to view the curriculum and align it with system and state frameworks. Some school districts have created their own curriculum plans that provide teachers with frameworks for teaching. Check with your cooperating teacher to see whether your school has developed these plans. Short-term planning includes unit plans, weekly plan-book plans, and daily lesson plans.

During your student teaching experience, you most likely will participate only in short-term planning. Ask your cooperating teacher to share her planning strategies with you. Ask how her plans are reviewed by her department chair or principal. This chapter will provide a variety of daily lesson plan formats. Select one that meets the needs of your classroom or design a format of your own. You *must* do lesson plans and share them with the cooperating teacher and university supervisor. Create a system for having your plans reviewed prior to teaching. For example, unit plans can be reviewed prior to teaching any of the lessons in the unit. As you teach the unit, daily plans will be created to meet the objectives you have stated. Weekly plan-book plans should be shared the week before you teach. These are short overviews mapping out the whole week showing what you will be teaching and when. They typically do not include goals, objectives, materials, and so on. Daily plans are the one-page sheets that have a more detailed script of the lesson and materials that you will need.

As you begin your teaching, all lessons you teach should be planned using the daily lesson plan form. Use the model plan, a sample from your grade level, or create your own planning format. All plans serve as an outline for your lesson and can be shared with your cooperating teacher before you teach the lesson. The plan allows you to think about your objectives for teaching before you teach. As you move through the semester, your cooperating teacher will assign more teaching and you will become more comfortable in understanding the components of a lesson. Use the unit plan guide, the weekly plan-book plan format, and the daily lesson plan sheets throughout your student teaching semester to document your teaching experience.

Student teachers often ask, "How many one-page daily forms do I have to do?" "Do I have to write a full-page plan for every lesson I teach?" "Do my plans have to be typed?" "When can I stop full plans and just complete plan-book style plans?" The answers to all these questions depend on the college requirements for obtaining a teacher license, the ability of the student teacher to think about and implement lessons, and the number of classes the student teacher is actually teaching. Daily lesson plans should not have to be typed unless they are being used in a unit that is being presented as part of your exit requirements. Make multiple copies of any of the forms from this chapter and simply handwrite your plan when you are working with your cooperating teacher. If the supervisor requires a typed copy for midterm and final observations, type those lessons. Talk with both your cooperating teacher and university supervisor to meet the lesson plan requirement for your student teaching program.

Student teachers often think every lesson in their student teaching binder has to be their own original created lesson. This is not the case. You may be coplanning lessons with your cooperating teacher, using plans designed by the textbook company, or following a fairly structured guide that has little room for change. You still need to write out the daily lesson plan for yourself so the plan does not say "Read Chapter 2 as the learning objective," but rather, you must state exactly what you are looking for as an outcome. All lessons handwritten or typed along with weekly plan books and units should be labeled, dated, and placed in your student teaching binder to be shared with your university supervisor on a regular basis.

Remember that plans are meant to be revised, reworked, redesigned, and adjusted to meet the needs of the learners. The plan is not the "goal," but rather the goal is to create a plan that promotes "teaching for understanding." Writing the plan is not the end result.

Make time every day for planning! It will make a difference in your teaching and your students' learning outcomes!

Using Prior Knowledge

What do you already know about lesson planning?

Did your college preparation program provide you with a planning template?

Do you know how to plan a unit? If "yes," where did you learn? If "no," who will help you?

Who will assist you in developing daily lesson plans?

What are the elements of a good plan? List them here.

Discuss the lesson plan format with your cooperating teacher. How does her format differ or compare to what you know about planning?

Discussing Professional Standards

*QUALITY CONVERSATIONS TO ENHANCE
STUDENT LEARNING*

National standards guide new teacher preparation in the United States. The INTASC created 10 principles for effective teaching. These principles are offered to you as a way to focus your attention on these key elements of practice. The "bottom line" is all about student learning. Are your students learning? How do you know?

Use these pages in each chapter to frame a quality conversation with your cooperating teacher and university supervisor. Don't be afraid to ask your own questions, too. Also use the REFLECT pages at the end of each chapter to deepen your thinking and to continue your quality conversations throughout the practium experience and into your first year of teaching.

INTASC Principles

Focus for Chapter 6

Discuss:

Principle #7   The teacher plans instruction based on knowledge of subject matter, students, the community, and curriculum goals.

Review:

Principle #1   The teacher understands the central concepts, tools of inquiry, and structures of the discipline(s) he or she teaches and can create learning experiences that make these aspects of subject matter meaningful for students.

Principle #2   The teacher understands how children learn and develop, and can provide learning opportunities that support their intellectual, social, and personal development.

ASK YOURSELF   What do these principles mean to me right now? How will I know if I have achieved these principles?

*DISCUSS WITH YOUR SUPERVISOR
OR COOPERATING TEACHER*

How will your supervisor/cooperating teacher know if you have achieved these principles? What evidence will you have to demonstrate these skills to them?

How will you know if your students have learned as a result of your teaching?

PLAN

USE ADVICE FROM FORMER STUDENT TEACHERS

Talk to student teachers who have just completed the experience and review the tips below to guide you.

- Focus on your students! Listen to them. Ask them questions. Modify your plans to meet their learning needs. Ask yourself: Are my students learning?
- Revise your plans as needed. Modify for students with special needs.
- Prepare plans that have extra activities at the end of the class for those students who might finish early.
- Visit the Internet websites in the chapter to discover new lesson plans.
- Notice how good planning impacts student behavior in your classroom!

PROCESS YOUR EXPERIENCE

Respond to the Key Questions below by completing the process pages in each chapter. These ACTs will encourage you to deepen your thinking about teaching and learning. Write on the pages and save them to review at the end of the experience.

KEY QUESTIONS

1. What types of planning are required of teachers?

2. What should I think about before I begin to plan?

3. What is ineffective planning?

4. How do I write objectives for effective lesson plans?

5. How do I create lesson plans from my cooperating teacher's ideas?

6. How do I use my time to teach lessons?

7. What are some good examples of daily lesson plans?

8. How should a weekly plan book be organized?

9. How do I design a curriculum unit?

10. How can I plan for successful learning outcomes?

PLAN

TAKE CARE OF YOURSELF AND AVOID STRESS

Plan to avoid the typical stresses of student teaching by following advice from cooperating teachers and university supervisors.

CONFRONT YOUR WORRIES!

Part of caring for yourself is recognizing what isn't working or what is worrying you about student teaching. Complaining, staying up nights, or being negative simply don't make you feel any better. But teaching is difficult and it is not always a perfect day. Recognize your worries and confront them by writing them down. Talk with your cooperating teacher and/or university supervisor about any worries. It is all right to keep track of what is "bugging" you!

What worries, concerns, or complaints will you list in your journal?

PLAN YOUR WEEK

Priority List

Done	Tasks	Priority	Complete by When?

Place things to do on the day you would like to do them.

Monday Date:	Tuesday Date:	Wednesday Date:	Thursday Date:	Friday Date:

CONNECT

CONNECT is a resource page with ideas and suggestions to support you during student teaching. Select and complete any CONNECT items that will enhance your experience in the classroom.

CONNECT with people

- Student teachers
  Talk with students who have completed student teaching. Ask them to share copies of lesson plans they found successful.

- Cooperating teacher(s)
  Review copies of plans the teacher has implemented in the past. Ask to see copies of plans from textbook companies or other resources.

CONNECT with readings & resources

- Books and authors to explore on the Internet or at your local library
  An Educator's Guide to Block Scheduling: Decision Making, Curriculum Design, and Lesson Planning Strategies by Bevevino et al. (Allyn and Bacon)
  Interdisciplinary High School Teaching by Clarke & Agne (Allyn and Bacon)
  Active Learning: 101 Strategies to Teach Any Subject by Silberman (Allyn and Bacon)
  The Power of Problem Solving: Practical Ideas for Any Subject K–8 by Sorenson et al. (Allyn and Bacon)
  Teaching & Learning Through Multiple Intelligences by Campbell et al. (Allyn and Bacon)

CONNECT technology to teaching

- Need lesson plans?
  Ask ERIC Lesson Plans = http://askeric.org/Virtual/Lessons/

- Check out other websites:
  Educator's Toolkit = http://www.eagle.ca/~matink
  Encarta Schoolhouse = http://encarta.msn.com/schoolhouse/default.asp
  Schrock School = http://school.discovery.com/schrockguide/index.html
  Sample worksheets = http://www.worksheetfactory.com
  English classes = http://www.englishteachersfile.com
  Biology classes = http://www.biologycorner.com

- Read
  A Guide to Integrating Technology into the Curriculum by Churma (Merrill)
  Internet Adventures by Leshin (Allyn and Bacon)

ACT
Process 6.1 Creating Lesson Plans from Cooperative Teacher's Ideas

At the beginning of your student teaching, the cooperating teacher will often suggest you teach part of a class or continue with a plan she may have already started. She may have had her students read a book and now she is asking you to create a review activity for the test that they will be having at the end of the week. You ask yourself, "Do I need a lesson plan to do this?" The answer is YES. The following suggestions will guide you.

- Select a planning form from this chapter that meets the needs of the lesson.

- Copy the plan format (make several copies in case you need to revise).

- Handwrite your objectives and procedures (pencil is best so you can erase and revise).

- Review the plan and check for accuracy and the time it will take.

- Show the plan to your cooperating teacher *before* you teach the lesson.

- Revise the plan to include any suggestions made by your cooperating teacher.

- Teach the lesson.

- Self-assess: *How did the plan work?*

- Ask your cooperating teacher for feedback: *What is the cooperating teacher's response to the lesson?*

- Record suggestions, attach to plan, and file in student teaching binder for future reference.

As a teacher, you will always be planning curriculum and designing lessons. As a student teacher, you may not participate in all aspects of planning because the cooperating teacher has probably done much of the long-range planning. Interview your cooperating teacher or department chair to determine how yearly and quarterly plans are designed and implemented. Take notes for future reference so you will be prepared to plan curriculum for your own classroom next year.

Use the examples in this chapter to guide your planning.

LONG-RANGE PLANS—YEARLY PLANNING
Purpose:

How were plans created?

What guides the plans?
    City/school system
    School or state curriculum guides
    Department
What does the plan look like?

LONG-RANGE PLANS—QUARTERLY PLANNING
(may be organized by marking term)
Purpose:

How were plans created?

What guides the plans?
    City/school system
    School or state curriculum guides
    Department
What does the plan look like?

SHORT-TERM PLANS—UNIT PLANNING

Short-term planning includes units, weekly plans, and daily lessons. It supports the goals of the long-term plans and puts into action these goals on a daily basis. Interview your cooperating teacher, department chair, or other teachers in the building to discover how they organize their short-term planning.

Units may be organized around themes or subject areas. Some units are interdisciplinary and use a variety of knowledge content areas. Units have a beginning and an end. See ACT Process 6.8 for suggestions on unit design.

- Review examples of "model" units from your school of education. How are they organized?

- Ask your cooperating teacher to share units she has completed. What do you notice?

SHORT-TERM PLANS—WEEKLY PLAN-BOOK PLANNING

Teachers commonly complete weekly plans in a plan book distributed by the school system. These books are often available in office supply stores, and you may want to purchase one to document the lesson you will be teaching during the week.

Another option is to copy a page from your teacher's plan book. Make multiple copies and place them in a three-ring binder to use as your own plan book. This will give you a complete documentation of all lessons you have taught.

- How is your cooperating teacher's plan book organized?

- Is it color coded? Could it be?

- How will you organize your plan book?

SHORT-TERM PLANS—DAILY LESSON PLANNING

Daily lesson plans stem from long-range planning and short-term planning goals. Examples of daily lesson plans are located in ACT Process 6.1 of this chapter.

- Does your cooperating teacher ever have a need for a daily plan?

- How did he do his daily plans when he was student teaching?

- What is the value to the daily plan in the scheme of long- and short-term planning?

ACT
Process 6.3   Daily Lesson Plans—What Do I Need to Know?

- **Why am I teaching this lesson?**
  Required curriculum?
  Student interest in topic?
  Your interest in topic?

- **What do I hope to accomplish?**
  Skill to be developed?
  Concept to be discussed for understanding?
  Product to be produced?

- **Who are the students?**
  Range of abilities?
  Range of ages?
  Ethnic diversity and varying cultures?

- **What is the time frame for teaching this lesson?**
  Part of a unit?
  One period or block schedule?
  Isolated lesson?

- **How will I begin the lesson to capture student attention?**
  Story, anecdote?
  Relevance to their lives?
  Props or visual displays?

- **Will I need other resources to teach this lesson?**
  Audiovisual or technology?
  Student handouts?
  Manipulatives or visual displays?

- **How will students spend their time during the lesson?**
  Small-group discussion? Individual? Large group?
  Hands-on activity or experiment?
  Taking notes or observing?

- **How will this lesson be assessed?**
  Formal? Quiz or test?
  Informal? Observation of learning?
  Open-ended questions? Written? Verbal?

- **How will I close the lesson and close the class period?**
  Review and summary?
  Collecting papers? Giving next assignment?
  Allowing time for homework or questions?

- **Will there be homework or enrichment activities offered?**
  How will I collect later? Is it required or extra?
  Will it count? What is cooperating teacher's policy?
  How will I grade it?

- **How will I know whether I succeeded in teaching the lesson?**
  Self-assessment?
  Response of students?
  Cooperating teacher input?

- **How will the next lesson relate or build on this one?**

- **What do I need to know about lesson planning?**

ACT
Process 6.4 Planning for Student Understanding

A teacher knows he has a good plan when at the end of the lesson or unit there is evidence of student understanding or skill development. An effective teacher, like an architect, designs a plan that will create a solid foundation for creative and original thinking. Teachers present information not just to be memorized for the weekly test, but to be understood and integrated into a student's thinking. This is not an easy task, but one that should be kept in your awareness as you begin to plan lessons.

What do you want students to know, understand, and be able to do *as a result of your lesson?*

FIVE STEPS TO SUCCESSFUL LESSON PLANNING

1. ***Think about breadth or depth*** **as you design your lessons and units.**

   Are you aiming for breadth in your lessons (i.e., being able to connect this concept to other concepts or relevant experiences)?
   - Students explain why or why not
   - Students extend the concept to others
   - Students think about and give examples of similar concepts

   Are you aiming for depth in your lessons (i.e., looking more at the detail about this idea)?
   - Students question the information
   - Students analyze the facts
   - Students prove something

2. ***Set priorities*** **for assessing student growth in lessons and units.**

   What do you expect all students to be familiar with?
   - To be able to do in this class?
   - To really understand for lasting learning?

3. *Select measurement tools* to determine student understanding.

How will you know students understand?
- What do *all* students have to know? How will you know?
- What do *most* students have to know? How will you know?
- What will *some* students have to know? How will you know?

4. *Create meaningful learning experiences* that engage and support learning (not just busywork).

- **Motivate.** Have you included a "hook" to gain attention and provide relevance?
- **Questions.** Do you have key questions that promote discussion and thinking?
- **Practice.** Do you have time for students to practice and engage in activity?
- **Self-Assessment.** Do you allow students time to reflect on their work and set goals?

5. *Observe what you are doing* during a class period.

If Teacher Does This...	*Students Respond This Way...*
Lectures and talks from front of class	Give short answers, take notes, listen
Promotes cooperative learning using • Inquiry • Seminar circles • Discussion • Open-ended questions	Collaborate in groups or pairs Question, revise, brainstorm Construct meaning

What are other ways in which you can assess your skills in lesson planning?

ACT
Process 6.5 Writing Teaching Objectives for Effective Lessons

Objectives state what the teacher wants the students to accomplish on completion of the lesson. Students should be clear about objectives before they begin the lesson so they know what is expected of them. Objectives should be written as one sentence.

Use verbs to write your lesson plan objectives. *Bloom's Taxonomy* organizes the verbs by levels of understanding beginning with basic knowledge and moving up through comprehension, application, analysis, synthesis, and evaluation. Higher-level thinking is expected for verbs at levels 5 and 6. These verbs indicate *what the student should be doing*. This taxonomy is applicable to all grade levels.

As you write your lesson plan objectives, select a verb and complete the sentence to state what is to be accomplished. State the objective in clear, understandable terms that can easily be understood by students and parents. Be sure to vary the levels of complexity in your lessons.

Examples: Name the planets, in order from the sun.
Predict the ending to this story.
Explain the reasons for the start of the Civil War.

Level of Thinking	Verbs
6 Evaluation	choose, conclude, evaluate, defend, rank, support, rate, etc.
5 Synthesis	construct, create, formulate, revise, write, plan, predict, etc.
4 Analysis	analyze, classify, compare, contrast, debate, categorize, etc.
3 Application	apply, demonstrate, draw, show, solve, illustrate, etc.
2 Comprehension	describe, explain, paraphrase, summarize, rewrite, etc.
1 Knowledge	define, identify, label, list, memorize, spell, name, etc.

What do you, in the role of the teacher, *need to do* to have the students experience a variety of learning objectives at all levels?

Remember, an effective teacher teaches so students meet the objectives stated in the lesson plan.

ACT
Process 6.6 Ineffective Lesson Planning
What Does Not Work?

If you are thinking...

How can I keep the students quiet?

What should I do today?

What can I use from the teacher's edition?

How can I get through this period?

What can I use for busywork?

Should I show a movie this period?

...You are not creating lessons for learning.

If you are only creating lessons such as...

Read Chapter 2 silently.

Complete this worksheet.

Do the problems on page 65.

Write a paragraph on _____.

...You are not teaching and planning lessons for student participation.

This kind of thinking and lesson planning without other types of interaction leads to frustration and poorly designed assignments. Assignments should state what the student will accomplish or achieve when the assignment is *complete,* not be an activity to keep the classroom quiet.

What is your personal experience of *ineffective* lesson planning?

How can you plan lessons that promote understanding?

ACT
Process 6.7   Time and Planning

One of the biggest concerns teachers have about teaching is that they don't have enough time in the day to do all there is to do. The majority of the time spent in class should be on teaching the curriculum that you have planned, not on making announcements, collecting lunch money, passing out materials, getting students into groups, or cleaning up. However, these tasks do need to get done.

A class period is your "allocated teaching time," but it also needs to include housekeeping activities. "Instructional time" is the time when students are actually engaged in learning activities. Your lesson plan is the way to organize your thinking so that most of the allocated time is spent engaging students in learning and checking for understanding.

Allocated Class Time: How Much Should You Spend?

How much time?	Start of Class Period Housekeeping Activities	• Required tasks • Collection of homework
Time?	BEGINNING LESSON Introducing or connecting to previous day	• Motivation/relevance • Overview • Directions • Purpose of lesson
Time?	Middle	• Objective • Key questions • Students engaged in learning • Activity • Knowledge • Student sharing • Informal assessment and checking for understanding
Time?	Closing	• Wrap up • Review of key points • Collection of materials/papers
Time?	Ending Class Period Housekeeping Activities	• Required tasks • Collection of classwork

Use this as a guide and include *time* as a factor in designing your lesson plans. When you have a particularly complicated lesson with many materials or if you need to move students into groups, take that into consideration and think of ways to prepare and set up so you don't take away from teaching time.

ACT
Process 6.8　General Guidelines for Unit Design

A unit is an organized group of lesson plans with a beginning, various activities, and a culmination. The unit may be subject based, interdisciplinary, or thematic. It can last as long as a semester or as short as a week. It has overarching themes and concepts to be learned through daily lessons. Teachers typically organize their teaching in teaching units by skills for early childhood, by subjects or themes for elementary/middle, or by subject area topics at secondary levels. Units are organized around books students have read, historical wars, science themes, topics, or anything you can think of that relates to knowledge.

A unit will have a general outline or plan for implementation and the daily lesson plans that demonstrate in detail how the unit is to be implemented in the classroom. Lesson plans are created as you move through the unit, not ahead of time, because the original plan often changes.

QUESTIONS TO CONSIDER BEFORE BEGINNING A UNIT

- What is the purpose of the unit?
- How much time will the unit need? How many lessons?
- What do students already know?
- What would students like to learn or know?
- How will the unit be introduced?
- What are the key questions that need to be answered?
- Is prior knowledge necessary?
- Will the unit have a theme?
- Will the unit cross disciplines? Is team teaching involved?
- Will any special activities be part of the unit?
- Will I need special materials or audiovisual for this unit?
- Will guest speakers or field trips be part of the unit?
- Other?

Check your university models for units and review units you have learned about in methods courses.

How will you organize your unit for student teaching?

What would you like to include for lesson activities in your unit?

UNIT ORGANIZERS

Unit organizers are valuable ways to map out your unit. Ask your cooperating teacher and university supervisor to share examples of unit organizers with you that can serve as models for your unit outline.

Title of Unit				
Purpose	Objectives	Key Questions	Key Vocabulary	Materials
Assessments	Possible Daily Lesson Activities	Opening Activity	Culmination	Guests or Trips

Another way to organize is a web. Adapt this example to web your unit.

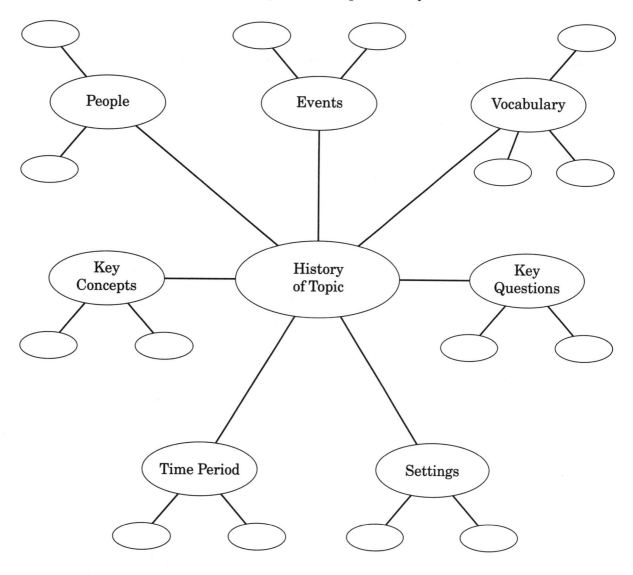

LESSON PLAN TITLE: Write the name of the topic or class here
DATE: Day you teach lesson

TIME OF CLASS: Period or time   **LENGTH OF PERIOD:** How much time to teach

SUBJECT: Content

PURPOSE OF LESSON: Why are you teaching this lesson? What is the goal you are seeking to reach?

OBJECTIVE: Bloom's taxonomy verb—what the student will achieve or accomplish

THEME OR UNIT #____: Is this an isolated lesson or part of a bigger curriculum unit? Number it as to where it fits in the sequence. If there is an expectation that students need prior knowledge to complete the lesson, how will you handle this with new students or those who have missed?

KEY QUESTIONS: The questions you will introduce to the students to guide the discussion and activities of the lesson should be broadly designed to encourage discussion and critical thinking. (Questions should not be designed with a yes-or-no answer.)

PROCEDURE: Note that the class period includes other housekeeping activities, such as collecting papers from the night before, announcing future school activities, or collecting lunch money. These need to be incorporated into the lesson plan to avoid running out of teaching time.

CLASSROOM MANAGEMENT NOTE: Effective planning ensures efficient teaching with a minimum of classroom discipline issues. Note any problems you foresee as you implement this lesson. For example, if you are using many supplies and students need to leave their seats, you need to be prepared to supervise this to avoid problems.

ASSESSMENT TOOL: What are you planning to use to check for understanding? List it here. Does it need to be collected?

FOLLOW-UP: Are there any ending details that need to be put on the board or announced at the end of class, such as homework assignments, extra credit options, or enrichment activities?

STUDENT TEACHER SELF-ASSESSMENT: What is your impression of the lesson and what would you do differently next time you teach it? Write your response on the back of the lesson plan.

Sample Procedure for Use of Allotted Classroom Time

Time	Classroom lesson	Teacher Behaviors: What will you be doing?	Expected Student Behaviors: What will the students be doing?
5%	Starting class period	Housekeeping	Listening Passing in homework
10%	Beginning lesson	Introducing objectives, vocabulary, and key questions	Showing interest Participating Listening
70%	Middle of Lesson	Facilitating a variety of activities for student learning	Collaborating Thinking, discussing Responding to key questions
10%	Closing lesson	Summarizing and reviewing lesson Setting goals for next lesson	Answering key questions Self-assessing
5%	Ending class period	Housekeeping	Passing in materials

ACT
Process 6.9B Lesson Plan Template
Sample Lesson Plan for Early Childhood

Date: _____   Subject: _____   Unit Lesson #:_____

OBJECTIVES FOR LESSON

1. _____

2. _____

Skills	Materials	Assessment
		What will *all* students learn?
		What will *most* students learn?
		What will *some* students learn?

ACT
Process 6.9C Lesson Plan Template
Sample Lesson Plan for All Levels

Lesson Plan Title: _____ **Date:**_____

Time of Class: _____ **Length of Period:** _____ **Subject:**_____

Purpose of Lesson: _____

Objective(s): _____

Theme(s): _____

KEY QUESTIONS

1. _____

2. _____

3. _____

KEY WORDS

1. _____ 4. _____

2. _____ 5. _____

3. _____ 6. _____

Classroom Management Notes: _____

_____

Assessment Tool: _____

_____

Follow-up/HW: _____

After the lesson, complete these questions.

How did the lesson go?

What will I do differently next time?

Tomorow I need to _____

Procedure

Time	Classroom Lesson	Teacher Behaviors: What will you be doing?	Expected Student Behaviors: What will the students be doing?
	Starting Class Period	Housekeeping	
	Beginning Lesson	Motivation/Key Questions	
	Middle of Lesson	Activities	
	Closing Lesson	Review	
	Ending Class Period	Housekeeping	

ACT
Process 6.9D Lesson Plan Template
Sample Lesson Plan for Elementary / Middle

Why Am I Teaching This Lesson?_____

Lesson Topic: _____

Curriculum Framework: _____

Subject: _____ **Date:**_____

BEHAVIORAL OBJECTIVES (What do you expect students to know and be able to do?)

1. _____
2. _____
3. _____

Key Vocabulary		*Key Questions*
1. _____ 4. _____		1. _____
2. _____ 5. _____		2. _____
4. _____ 6. _____		3. _____

Materials/resources/technology:

Procedure (beginning, middle, closing):

Assessment (How will I know students learned?):

Classroom management notes/Lesson modifications:

Homework/Follow-up/Enrichment:

TEACHER SELF-ASSESSMENT OF LESSON

What would I do differently? (Write on back or attach.)

ACT
Process 6.9E Lesson Plan Template
Sample Plan for Secondary

Why Am I Teaching This Lesson? _____

Date: _____   **Period:** _____   **Time:** _____

Curriculum Framework: _____

Subject: _____   **Block:** _____

Objectives	*Key Questions*
1. _____ _____	1. _____ _____
2. _____ _____	2. _____ _____
3. _____ _____	3. _____ _____

Vocabulary:

_____ _____ _____

_____ _____ _____

_____ _____ _____

_____ _____ _____

_____ _____ _____

Textbook: _____   **Pages:** _____

Material/Handouts: _____

Introduction:	Overview (Purpose of Lesson) (What do I expect students to know and be able to do?):
Mini-Lecture:	Key points:
Student pairs, group work, or way in which students are engaged:	Activities:
Closing:	Summary:

Assessment:

Homework:

ACT
Process 6.9F Lesson Plans
Creating My Own Plan

Label the blocks to meet your needs.

Date: _____ **Subject:** _____

REFLECT

Three ways you may use to reflect on your practice during student teaching are listed on this page. Select the methods of reflection that will stimulate your thinking. Write in an *Inquiry Journal* during student teaching. This writing will serve as a data source for solving problems over time. Uncover your own assumptions, biases, and dispositions as you write in your journal several times each week.

✓ **Inquiry: Teacher Research as a Tool for Solving Classroom Problems and Enhancing Student Learning**

What questions are arising as you think about designing daily lesson plans that will focus on student learning. What is difficult for you as you design lessons?

_____

_____

_____

_____

Review the *Key Questions* in the PLAN section of this chapter. Which questions are still confusing? List them below and set up a time to discuss them with your cooperating teacher or supervisor.

_____

_____

_____

✓ **Self-Reflection: Analyze Your Teaching Strategies to Enhance Student Learning** (Use the processes in Chapter 3 to guide your self-reflection.)

Which lesson plan template will you be using?_____

Why did you select this format? _____

_____

Which lessons will you reflect on for mid-term and final observations?

_____

_____

_____

✓ **Critique: Feedback from Your Supervisor and Cooperating Teacher to Guide Your Planning, Instructional Practice, and Professionalism**

What are your cooperating teacher and supervisor suggesting as good strategies for behavior management and discipline?

_____

_____

_____

Chapter 7

Instructional Strategies for Diverse Learners

How Do I Teach to Varied Student Needs?

Take time to connect with your generation of future colleagues—your classmates and other student teachers. Take the time to connect with them personally and professionally. Share strategies and ideas for teaching lessons to diverse learners. It will broaden your perspective and prepare you for your own classroom. Don't take the easy way out —try lots of new strategies!

Student Teacher

A successful teacher is one who can observe and recognize the varying needs in her classroom and create meaningful learning opportunities for all her students. This chapter builds on the key questions introduced in previous chapters related to observation, classroom management, and lesson planning. Who are the students in the class? What do they think of each other? How do they interact? Who are you as a teacher? What is your comfortable style of teaching? How do you reach out to students with various learning abilities? All these questions affect the way in which you present curriculum and how students respond to learning.

Diversity can be defined in many ways. Race, gender, ethnicity, religious beliefs, academic ability, personality, physical ability, habits, fears, and family support vary from student to student. What is the cultural makeup of this school? Who are the students? Do they have special education needs? How culturally diverse is your class? With cultural diversity comes multiple perspectives, global awareness, and responsibility to discuss issues of world significance. The students in the classroom bring the world to the classroom, and they can become an integral component in the learning community. Cultural diversity also may bring other needs, such as language. Diversity defined in this broad way illustrates that *all* students are diverse and that teaching to varying needs in today's classroom is a complex task.

Your own teaching and learning styles relate to how you choose to present instructional strategies to your students. How much do you know about your teaching style? Do you know how you prefer to teach? What is your learning style? How will you learn the preferred learning styles of the students in your classroom? What is your cooperating teacher's style? Are you similar or different in your approaches? Discuss teaching and learning styles with your cooperating teacher and supervisor to gain more insight into your style and the importance of matching your style with your students' learning needs and the state and district standards.

Become familiar with the current information that shapes the thinking of the educational community. As you participate in student teaching, you will hear many "buzz words" and "hot topics" as teachers plan and discuss practice. Some of these include performance assessment, differentiated instruction, inclusion, multiple intelligences, block scheduling, rubrics, outcomes based-instruction, time and learning, brain-based learning, communities of learners, data-driven decisions, instructional technology, performance standards, and more. This chapter will highlight some of these topics. This is just the beginning of your learning curve! Don't be afraid to ask what terms mean if you do not understand what is being discussed.

Use the processes in this chapter to begin to practice some of the key areas that you need to know and be able to do as you develop as a teacher. You don't have to master all of these approaches and strategies at this time! This is just the beginning. Listen, learn, and build on the knowledge bases established in your curriculum methods courses.

Curriculum, instruction, and *assessment* are the building blocks for teaching. As you design curriculum and create daily plans and longer units, keep in mind how this content will connect your students to the world beyond the classroom.

Components of Effective Teaching	Description
Curriculum. The expected learning outcomes for the school, district, and state. The curriculum is made up of daily lessons and longer units of study.	**WHAT** you teach and **WHAT** is expected to be learned by students
Instruction. How the curriculum is presented to students using a variety of instructional strategies. Teachers learn through professional development and add to their "repertoire" of strategies that enhance student learning of curriculum.	**HOW** you teach
Assessment. How you measure what students know and can do as a result of the instruction. Informal and formal assessments as well as high-stakes evaluations in the district or state provide data for curriculum or instruction revision.	**HOW** you know that students have learned

Students have many skills and needs that surface in a classroom. By providing rich and varied approaches to teaching any lesson, you will have a better chance of meeting these needs and going beyond them. Variety and alternatives keep the classroom exciting and the students interested.

Discussing Professional Standards

QUALITY CONVERSATIONS TO ENHANCE STUDENT LEARNING

National standards guide new teacher preparation in the United States. The INTASC created 10 principles for effective teaching. These principles are offered to you as a way to focus your attention on these key elements of practice. The "bottom line" is all about student learning. Are your students learning? How do you know?

Use these pages in each chapter to frame a quality conversation with your cooperating teacher and university supervisor. Don't be afraid to ask your own questions, too. Also use the REFLECT pages at the end of each chapter to deepen your thinking and to continue your quality conversations throughout the practium experience and into your first year of teaching.

INTASC Principles

Focus for Chapter 7

Discuss:

Principle #3   The teacher understands how students differ in their approaches to learning and creates instructional opportunities that are adapted to diverse learners.

Principle #4   The teacher understands and uses a variety of instructional strategies to encourage students' development of critical thinking, problem solving and performance skills.

Review:

Principle #2   The teacher understands how children learn and develop, and can provide learning opportunities that support their intellectual, social, and personal development.

Principle #7   The teacher plans instruction based on knowledge of subject matter, students, the community, and curriculum goals.

ASK YOURSELF   What do these principles mean to me right now? How will I know if I have achieved these principles?

DISCUSS WITH YOUR SUPERVISOR OR COOPERATING TEACHER

How will your supervisor/cooperating teacher know if you have achieved these principles? What evidence will you have to demonstrate these skills to them?

How will you know if your students have learned as a result of your teaching?

PLAN

USE ADVICE FROM FORMER STUDENT TEACHERS

Talk to student teachers who have just completed the experience and review the tips below to guide you.

- Experiment with a variety of strategies and ask the students which ones helped them learn the information.
- Don't forget to integrate the arts and multiple intelligences to offer your student many approaches.
- Use problem-solving techniques and open-ended questions to enrich lessons.

PROCESS YOUR EXPERIENCE

Respond to the Key Questions below by completing the process pages in each chapter. These ACTs will encourage you to deepen your thinking about teaching and learning. Write on the pages and save them to review at the end of the experience.

KEY QUESTIONS

1. Who are the students in my classroom?

2. How do preferred teaching and learning styles define my classroom?

3. How can I give directions so that all students understand what to accomplish?

4. When do I teach to the whole class or use small groups?

5. How do I modify lessons for students with special needs?

6. Which materials should I be using in my classroom?

7. How do questions promote higher-order thinking?

8. What about extra credit and homework?

9. Should students ever have a choice about assignments?

10. What is service learning and how does it relate to teaching?

PLAN

TAKE CARE OF YOURSELF AND AVOID STRESS

Plan to avoid the typical stresses of student teaching by following advice from cooperating teachers and university supervisors.

SEE THE WORLD AROUND YOU!

What do you see that makes you feel good about beginning this day?

What is pleasing about your school and school surroundings?

What is positive about the students with whom you are working?

After you have acknowledged the pleasant things, decide to add some beauty to your school or classroom. Get your students to participate, too!

If you have a permanent classroom, select one or more of the following:

- Hang student artwork in a visible location.
- Buy flowers or a plant for the classroom (and the teachers' room).
- Grow something in the classroom that is beautiful.
- Hang posters and pictures that are pleasing to look at.
- Collect positive news stories and post them.

PLAN YOUR WEEK

Priority List

Done	Tasks	Priority	Complete by When?

Place things to do on the day you would like to do them.

Monday Date:	Tuesday Date:	Wednesday Date:	Thursday Date:	Friday Date:

CONNECT

CONNECT is a resource page with ideas and suggestions to support you during student teaching. Select and complete any CONNECT items that will enhance your experience in the classroom.

CONNECT with people

- Speakers on diversity topics
  Attend any events that give you an opportunity to listen and learn about diverse learners and diversity issues.

CONNECT with readings & resources

- Books and authors to explore on the Internet or at your local library
  An Introduction to Multicultural Education by Banks *(Allyn and Bacon)*
  Teacher Talk: Multicultural Lesson Plans by Eldridge (Allyn and Bacon)
  Open Minds to Equality: A Sourcebook of Learning Activities to Affirm Diversity and Promote Equity by Schniedewind and Davidson (Allyn and Bacon)
  Why Are All the Black Kids Sitting Together in the Cafeteria? by Tatum (Basic Books)
  Other People's Children by Delpit (New Press)

CONNECT technology to teaching

- Surf the Net to chat about or find great lessons for diverse learners of all levels. Use Yahoo, Netscape, People Search, Alta Vista, or Electric Library to search.
- Check out websites
  Site for teaching students with special needs = http://parentpals.com/gossamer/pages/
  Scholastic = http://www.scholastic.com
  Multicultural Book Review = http://www.isomedia.com/homes/jmele/homepage.html
  NEA (National Education Association) = http://www.nea.org/cet
  National Coalition for Equality in Learning = http://www.umass.edu/soe/ncel/
  Site for students to reinforce skills learned in class at home = http://www.cogcon.com/gamegoo/gooeyhome.html

ACT
Process 7.1 Getting to Know My Students

An important aspect of teaching is knowing your students. You began the process in Chapter 4 by creating a class profile. Continue the process through observation, surveys, and interviews. Listening to your students, understanding their needs, and responding to their suggestions are all ways to build relationships. Student teachers have shared that being too much like a friend instead of a teacher in the beginning of the student teaching led to difficulty when they had to take over the teacher role later in the term. This doesn't mean, however, that you can't be pleasant or friendly!

Some ways to continue to learn about your students...

1. **Create an Interest Survey.** Ask students to complete a short-answer survey. Here are some sample questions to adapt for elementary or secondary students:
   - What do you like most about school?
   - Do you have an after-school job?
   - How do you learn best?
   - What is your favorite subject? Do you participate in extra curricula?
   - What language do you speak at home?
   - Have you ever traveled to another country?
   - What could I help you learn this year?
   - What do you wish you could do in school?
   - What is your favorite sport or hobby? Do you play sports?
   - Do you play a musical instrument? Are you in a band?
   - Do you do community service?

Adapt questions to meet the needs of your age group. You may have to read the questions to younger children and write their answers on the board, or they can circle a set of smile faces to show their opinion.

Short version: Select one or two questions and have students write the answers on the front and back of an index card. Make sure they write their name on the card!

Read the answers carefully and note the diverse needs and skills presented in this information. You may want to create a grid with names and skills to chart the whole class. Use this information to create a classroom profile.

2. **Take photographs of each student.** Students love it and it will help you learn their names and faces. This may be more appropriate for younger students. A whole-class photograph is fun for all age groups.

3. **Interview as many students as possible.** Ask them to talk about their experiences in school and how they feel they learn best. You may want to audiotape these talks for future reference. Be sure to get permission from cooperating teacher, student, and parent.

4. **Interview your cooperating teacher.** Ask him to identify students with special needs who will require modifications in their work and any other students who should be noted.

5. **What are your ideas for getting to know your students?**

ACT
Process 7.2 Learning Styles—How Do Students Learn?

Students learn in many ways. Being able to recognize the differences will assist you in designing lessons and bringing the students together as a team. Diversity of learning styles makes the team more resourceful, yet students also need to be aware of the differences so they don't argue about their different approaches.

Check your own preferred learning styles and compare with your cooperating teacher. Review current learning-style theories and translate that theory into practice by observing students. Many of these theorists have short learning-style tests that are available for use. Check with the school guidance counselor or adjustment counselor for details.

Ask the students how they think they learn best. Students know what they prefer and which methods work best for them. Think of ways to train students to build on their own learning strengths so they can adjust conditions to suit them. As a student teacher, you should be assisting students in becoming more comfortable with several learning styles.

1. Review your students to see which are primarily:

   ____Auditory   ____Visual   ____Hands-on   ____Random

   ____Sequential   ____Inductive   ____Deductive

   Most students are a combination of several but have a preferred approach.

2. Interview several students in the classroom about their preferred learning style. Ask the students why they prefer this style. If they use a combination, list them.

   STUDENT   **PREFERRED STYLE(S)**   **REASON**

   _____   _____   _____

   _____   _____   _____

   _____   _____   _____

3. Note current learning-style theory here and list any key points that will assist you in teaching.

   _____

   _____

ACT
Process 7.3   Teaching Styles—Which Do I Prefer?

An awareness level of your teaching style and how it matches your students' learning styles is important as you begin to teach lessons. Students may demonstrate a variety of "intelligences" and teachers need to be aware of them.

Do you like to talk and explain concepts to students verbally?
Then you probably...
> ...lecture for a major part of the class period.
> ...talk to students.

Students who prefer auditory learning will respond.

Do you like to write and see concepts on paper?
Then you probably...
> ...use the board to list ideas.
> ...write outlines for students.
> ...create study guides.
> ...ask students to take notes.

Students who prefer to see things in writing will respond.

Do you enjoy using visual displays?
Then you probably...
> ...use the computer to demonstrate a concept.
> ...bring in models and posters to show students.
> ...use webbing and graphic organizers.

Students who prefer pictures and drawings will respond.

Do you like to touch and see things happen?
Then you probably...
> ...create experiments for your classroom.
> ...design hands-on lessons with manipulatives.
> ...bring things to show and tell about.

Students who want to touch and observe the activity will respond.

As you begin student teaching, you may discover that you enjoy and actually demonstrate all these styles in your classroom or that one mode of presenting is your preferred and comfortable style. Students in your classroom will have a variety of learning and preferred styles. Once you discover their styles and multiple intelligences, you will need to be sure that you adapt and vary your teaching so that all students will respond. Remember, the goal is to have students learn to respond to as many styles of teaching as possible, not to select one. You may have to teach them how to respond as well as teach the material.

How would you describe your preferred style?

ACT
Process 7.4   Giving Directions to Diverse Learners

Observe your cooperating teacher as he gives directions to the class. How does he state the directions? Does he present them in a variety of ways to accommodate all the learners? How will you present directions when you are teaching? Notice how you prefer to receive directions when you are learning something new. Ask your students how they need to receive directions.

How does your cooperating teacher give directions?
Verbal: Are they clear? How long does it take to give them? Did they have several steps?
Visual: Are they written on the board, overhead, or given to students?

What does his voice sound like when giving directions?
Volume: Can the directions be heard at the back of the room?
Pronunciation: Are the words pronounced correctly?
Articulation: How clearly are words expressed?
Speed: Are key points spoken slowly enough for all to understand?

Where is the teacher in the classroom when giving directions?
Position: Where did the teacher stand? Was he sitting?
Movement: Did the teacher move around to check on the students?

What else did you notice about the teacher when he gave directions?
Clarification: Did he allow opportunities for students to ask clarifying questions?
What else did you notice?

How can complicated directions create problems for students who may be learning-challenged?

What can you do to avoid potential problems related to poor directions?

ACT
Process 7.5 Whole-Class Instruction—
Lectures and Presentations

The most common practices in whole-class instruction are described in the following table. The problem with whole-group strategies is that the students are often "passive" participants in the process. When using these strategies, check for understanding throughout the lesson.

Strategy	*Purpose*
Lecture	Introducing unit or lesson, sharing a personal experience, summarizing a lesson or unit, providing information that students could not learn any other way, describing a problem, etc.
Class Discussion	Creating questions that relate to the lecture and posing them to class during or after lecture
Demonstration Lesson	Visually presenting an experiment or model for class to show "how" something should look
Simulation	Introducing or "hooking" students when introducing a new concept
Reading	Reading a passage, book, or poem to class to have them respond to, etc.

Observe your cooperating teacher using these methods and ask why she has selected a whole-group strategy. Many times, whole-class strategies are incorporated into a lesson for either the introduction or the closing of a lesson with small groups or paired learning in between.

Think about how you will incorporate whole-class strategies into you teaching. How can these strategies impact student learning? How will you know if students are learning in a large group?

ACT
Process 7.6   Flexible and Cooperative Learning Groups

Flexible grouping is a strategy for creating groups based on students' academic needs. *Flexible* means that the student is not "tracked" into this group for the whole year, but rather just works in this group until the skill is mastered. Groups change regularly, so that no students stay with the same tracked group or are labeled as being in low, middle, and high groups. New groups are formed as the class moves on to new skills or material. The teacher works with the group while other students work independently. The teacher rotates to all groups during the week and has an opportunity to work with all students in this smaller setting. This allows the teacher to check for understanding and to get closer to each student. Flexible-grouping strategies vary by grade level.

Cooperative learning is currently being used in a variety of formats in schools. Teachers have students work in pairs, triads, and small groups. Some teachers use the groups for project work; others use the pairs or groups to practice new skills with each other. The key to cooperative learning is that you have to "teach" the students how to work cooperatively *before* you can expect them to do it.

How does an "effective" cooperative group or pair look in your classroom?

If you or your cooperating teacher has never tried cooperative learning, start by pairing students.

For younger students, try using

- *Partners as coaches.* Let each student in the room select another student who will be his partner for support. When he is absent, this person can collect the papers for him all day. When he doesn't understand a concept, he can go to this person for help.
- *Paired learners.* Pair students with students who are like them in learning styles, need, or interests, and let them enjoy working together on a special activity.
- *High/low learners.* Let students who have grasped a concept work with students who have not.
- *Paired share.* In any class for two or more minutes, let the students turn to the person next to them and share something you have already set up.
- *Paired readers.* Either by choice or design, let students read aloud to each other.

For older students, ask them to

- Turn to the person next to them and share the answer to the question on the board.
- Read this page and answer the questions together.
- Predict what will come next and present it to the class together.
- Compare their homework and correct any errors before passing it in.

What are some other ways students can work in pairs?

How is cooperative learning different from flexible grouping?

ACT
Process 7.7   Differentiated Instruction for ALL Learners

Teachers have the power to create an environment in the classroom that has the potential for *all* students to learn and achieve a level of success. Students in a classroom enter at all levels. Some may be struggling learners, others are so advanced the teacher needs to set up alternative methods to keep their interest and bring them to higher levels of achievement.

Differentiated instruction means the teacher will provide:
1. Materials and readings that represent several reading levels
2. Choices for students as to "how" they will complete a task
3. A variety of possible product/process options that would provide evidence of learning by the students
4. A balance between whole class, pairs, small group, and individual learning

The teacher needs to pay attention to:
1. Readiness levels of students
2. Learning styles of students
3. Interests of students

Talk with your cooperating teacher about the learners in your classroom and how you can use differentiated instruction for struggling or advanced learners.

What will you do?

What do you see as the challenges of differentiated instruction? Why is it important as a teacher of *all* students to overcome them?

Howard Gardner's research on multiple intelligences has added a new approaches to working with diverse learners.

Review these and brainstorm activities with your cooperating teacher that would demonstrate ways your students could express their learning though their own "intelligences."

Intelligence	Possible Activities for Demonstrating Learning in the Classroom
Bodily/Kinesthetic—processing though touch, movement, drama	Learning centers, models, etc.,
Intra-personal—processing personally through reflection	Journals, goal setting, etc.,
Inter-personal—processing by sharing	Cooperative groups, teaching another student, etc.
Verbal/Linguistic—processing through reading, writing, speaking, listening	Discussions, etc.
Musical/Rhythmic—processing through rhythm, moods, melodies, sounds	Choral readings, lyrics, etc.
Logical/Mathematical—processing through numbers, patterns	Logic, story problems, etc.
Visual/Spatial—processing through images and visualizing	Charts, posters, video, etc.
Naturalist	Nature walks, knowing names of trees, seasons, weather, etc.
Existentialist	Philosophy—Big questions: "Who am I?" "Why am I here?"—religion, etc.

ACT
Process 7.9 Bloom's Taxonomy
Using Questions to Teach

Bloom's Taxonomy of thinking is listed from most complex to less complex.

Level	*Taxonomy*	*Example of Strategy*
6	**Evaluation**. Examine all parts of a concept to evaluate or asses the significance.	Read a passage and evaluate the author's message and present it.
5	**Synthesis**. Combine a new concept with what you already know to construct new knowledge.	Use the information given with your own ideas to pose an argument.
4	**Analysis**. Separate a new concept into its parts and understand the relationships.	Compare and contrast.
3	**Application**. Solve a problem by applying the knowledge learned.	Use the words in sentences, and make a chart to show what you learned.
2	**Comprehension**. Explain or restate the ideas.	Summarize in your own words.
1	**Knowledge.** Recognize and recall facts.	Memorize or recite.

Use the taxonomy to note the types of questions you are using in your lessons. Also note the types of questions your students are asking in class. Are your students asking questions during your lessons? Why or why not? Copy this chart and collect some data related to your use of questions.

Questions YOU Use in a Given Lesson	*How Many at Levels 4–6?*	*Questions YOUR STUDENTS Ask in a Lesson*	*How Many at Levels 4–6?*
Examples		Examples	

Strive to use higher levels of the Taxonomy in your lessons!

Note: Open-ended questions allow students to expand their thinking on a particular topic. They require more than a yes-or-no answer; they require the students to think about the issue in a more complex way. These questions would relate to the higher levels of Bloom's taxonomy.

You may ask open-ended questions as part of your introduction to a teaching unit and explain that students will be learning about this topic in such a way that this question will be answered.

Use the basic questions Who, What, Where, When, How, and Why to develop open-ended questions to bring your students to higher levels of thinking.

EXAMPLES OF OPEN-ENDED QUESTIONS

_____

_____

_____

_____

_____

Note: Open-ended questions can be part of your motivator to grab the students' attention and also be part of the assessment process at the end of the unit.

Review your textbooks and teacher's edition for examples of open-ended questions. Are questions categorized in your texts? Are questions at the rote knowledge/comprehension level or at higher levels?

Use KWL as a strategy to find out what students **K**now about the topic, what they **W**ant to know, and what they **L**earned (at the end of the unit).

Note: Don't forget to *ask the students* what their questions are before, during, and at the end of lessons and units. They can write them on index cards and leave them in a "Question Box" for you to answer at a later time. If you are receiving the same questions, you may want to clarify one of your objectives. Formulating good questions is challenging and an important skill for students to learn!

What types of questions are students asking in the classes you observe or teach?

ACT
Process 7.10 Brain-Based Learning
What Do I Need to Know?

Teachers are continuing to learn and understand how the brain works, as well as how they can use this information to present curriculum and instructional strategies to their students.

Talk with your cooperating teacher(s), university supervisor, and peers to see what they know about brain research.

Ten Concepts to Keep in Mind as You Prepare Lessons for Diverse Learners

1. Humans use only use a small part of the capacity of their brains.
2. Effective effort has more to do with success than does intelligence as it is currently measured in schools.
3. Learners are constantly trying to make meaning by looking for connections and patterns.
4. People learn best when they feel safe and reasonably sure that they will be successful.
5. People learn best when they can use the new information learned in a relevant way.
6. The search for meaning occurs through "patterning."
7. Learners' emotions are critical to patterning.
8. Learning involves conscious and unconscious processing.
9. Learning involves focus and peripheral attention.
10. Complex learning is enhanced by challenge an inhibited by threat.

What do you already know about brain research?

How will you use what you know in your classroom?

ACT
Process 7.11 Standards-Based Teaching
The Big Picture

Standards are being used in states and school districts to determine whether successful learning has taken place. These measures, or "outcomes," by students may determine funding or resources for schools. The federal No Child Left Behind Act stresses standards.

Standards apply to all students in a school but all students may not be able to achieve or demonstrate the standard in the same way. This is why teachers need a variety of instructional strategies to meet the needs of diverse learners.

Interview your cooperating teacher about state teaching and learning standards.

1. What are the standards or frameworks this school/teacher is using? How are they reflected in her planning? How are they impacted by her instructional strategies?

2. How does your cooperating teacher integrate school and/or state standards in her classes/classroom?

3. How were the standards established that are being used? Are they fair? Will all students be able to meet these standards?

4. What else do you need to know about standards and learning outcomes?

ACT
Process 7.12 Students with Special Needs
Individual Plans

Special education and *inclusion* are popular terms in schools today. How a teacher groups students with special needs within the classroom is important. Are the students part of the flexible or cooperative-grouping procedures? Ask your cooperating teacher how the school and district support students with special needs.

How much adapting will you have to do in your lessons to accommodate and enrich the lives of students who are dealing with physical or emotional challenges?

_____

_____

What do you already know about the students with special needs in your classroom?

_____

_____

What questions do you have?

_____

_____

Discuss with your cooperating teacher any students who have been identified as "at risk" in your classroom. Ask him to explain what the criteria are for determining the risk and to share the student's individualized education program.

List the students' names here if you need to review their IEPs (individualized education programs). Note that these plans may be confidential and that parents need to sign them. Review the plans for any learning adaptations you will have to integrate into your teaching.

_____   _____

_____   _____

Interview the special education director or teacher in your school.

SAMPLE QUESTIONS

Does the state have a law or policy relating to students with specials needs?

How is *special needs* defined in your state?

Is the school currently using "inclusion" and how does it work?

Are some students "pulled out" of classrooms for tutoring? How does this work?

What is the role of the teacher with special education inclusion models?

Are classroom teachers coteaching with special education teachers?

Notes: _____

_____

Students with academic special needs often have varying abilities. The lessons you design to meet the curriculum objectives may need to be modified or adapted to be in compliance with students' individualized education programs or to meet students at their own skill levels. Students think and work at different speeds. Some who finish quickly may not have actually understood the concept. Some who work more slowly may be thoughtful thinkers who see the complexity in every concept. Notice how the students in your classes complete their work. The fastest workers are not always the most accurate or most creative problem solvers. Don't get trapped into rewarding those who finish first. Always check for accuracy! Sometimes it doesn't matter whether the whole assignment is complete—you can check for understanding with what IS done and not use the incompleteness as a negative assessment of growth.

EXAMPLES OF MODIFICATIONS

- Giving a student more time to complete an assignment
- Assigning fewer questions or examples to be completed
- Allowing students to tape-record their answers instead of writing
- Working with a partner who would write the answers the student stated verbally
- Accepting printed work instead of cursive
- Using the computer to complete work

Interview your cooperating teacher and ask:

How do you know which activities you can leave incomplete and which have to be done?

How do you pace a lesson so that all or most students complete the task?

How do you create high expectations for learners who work more slowly?

Discuss with your cooperating teacher how lessons are currently being modified for individual students in your classroom. List the student and the modification in your lesson plans.

Student #1 _____ modification _____

Student #2 _____ modification _____

Student #3 _____ modification _____

Student #4 _____ modification _____

Student #5 _____ modification _____

In addition to reviewing files and individualized education programs (IEPs) of students with special needs, you should also observe the students during the school day. Use the forms from Chapter 2 to organize your thoughts and document your observations.

A daily observation for as little as 15 minutes can reveal significant information about a student's learning style and needs. Observe students in your classroom, on the playground, and in any other learning environment.

1. Shadow one of your students who has special needs for part of a school day.
    Ask yourself...
    Does the IEP match the student's needs in your opinion?
    Does the student behave differently
    on the playground? in the cafeteria? outside the building?
    in the large group? passing in the hallway?
    in small groups? in pairs?
    in another classroom setting, such as art, music, physical education?
    during instructional time? playing sports?
    What surprised you about the student?
    What is the student doing well?

2. Interview the student after you have completed your shadow observations.
    Ask the student...
    What does she like about school?
    What does she find difficult?
    How could you, as her teacher, assist her in learning?

Think about and discuss with your cooperating teacher or supervisor how this information can assist you in meeting the needs of other students who have special needs in your classroom.

ACT
Process 7.15 Enrichment and Homework
Should I? Will They?

ENRICHMENT

Enrichment can be offered to students who have a deeper interest in the topic or those who may complete classwork early (and accurately). Special activities in a learning center, questions on the board, or enrichment sheets provide opportunities for more connection to a particular topic.

Ask your cooperating teacher how she provides enrichment activities for gifted and talented students, students who complete work early, or students who have a genuine interest in this topic.

Ideas for enrichment:

_____

_____

Note: Enrichment should not just be a reward for those who complete their work early. Students who have varying paces may never have a chance to try more challenging activities offered. Create one day a month as "enrichment" period and let students select a topic they truly enjoy learning about. These topics could become "clubs" where students meet regularly to learn more about what they like.

HOMEWORK

Observe and interview your cooperating teacher about homework policies. Do students have to pass in homework? Is it always required? Does it only relate to the text? Do students get to select homework activities? Is homework extra credit? Does your cooperating teacher correct homework? If not, how does it count toward the grade? Is there such a thing as "creative" homework?

What are you ideas about using homework as part of the curriculum?

What happens if students don't do their homework? For example, they had to read a chapter in a book and you designed a lesson around the expectation that they had read it. What do you do about the planned lesson?

ACT
Process 7.16 Using Technology and Audiovisual Aids to Teach

Textbooks are often used as the basic curriculum for a classroom; however, they do not have to be the *only* resource that is used. Ask your cooperating teacher to share his opinion about the textbooks you will be using this semester. Review all the materials and teacher's editions that are part of the textbook series. How does the textbook relate to your school curriculum?

Audiovisual materials and computers can be an integral component in creating a rich teaching and learning environment. They also provide other ways for varied-learning-style students to approach a learning activity.

Review the list of materials and code them by your level of familiarity.

Key: C = comfortable with using this resource
       N = need to learn how to use this resource

C or N	Types of Material	Where I Might Integrate into My Teaching
	Audiovisual aids	
	Overhead projector	
	Computer/Computer lab	
	CD/CD-ROM	
	Video camera	
	VCR and TV/DVD	
	Tape recorder with headsets	
	Slide projector	
	LCD Projector/Laptop	
	Video recorder	
	Digital camera	

ACT
Process 7.17   Choices—Do Students Have Any?

Allow for student choice whenever possible. Students usually know how they learn best, and if you can offer them a variety of ways in which to show you that they know the material, they will feel more successful and will be more invested in the work.

Ask your cooperating teacher how he uses choice in the classroom. If he doesn't allow for choice, discuss how it might be used in limited, appropriate ways to provide opportunities for students.

Examples of ways choice can be incorporated into your classroom:

- Choosing a homework assignment from three that are acceptable
- Choosing a partner to work with on a project
- Choosing an independent reading book
- Choosing the type of test (multiple choice, essay, short answer)
- Creating a test by choosing all the items that would go on the test

List other ways to incorporate choice into your classroom that would promote student interest.

_____

_____

Example of how choice of strategy could be used to meet an objective:

To solve a particular work problem, students could choose to

- Use paper and pencil
- Use manipulatives
- Draw the answer
- Work alone
- Work with a partner
- Act out the answer

Can you think of ways in which you could provide your students with choice without disrupting curriculum and while supporting the needs of diverse learners?

_____

_____

ACT
Process 7.18 Service Learning
Contributing to the Community

Service learning is a way in which students in your classes can participate in the larger community. Ask your cooperating teacher whether the school or her classroom is currently participating in a service learning project. Sometimes high school students receive academic credit for their projects and actually work as interns in public jobs during the school day. Elementary students may visit nursing homes or shelters and read to people.

Connecting your students through the existing curriculum is a better way to include service than "adding" on another activity for already busy students. Service learning engages students and makes the curriculum come alive for all learners. Service projects can also be offered as enrichment, extra credit, and homework for those students who are committed to making a difference.

Examples of service learning activities:

History, middle/high	Interview and audiotape World War II veterans and then have them come to the classroom as guest speakers. Provide a service to the local veterans' association as part of this activity.
Science, middle/high	Connect with a recycling center on a project that relates to the science chapter on recycling.
Elementary	Write to the elderly and visit them on holidays; use as language arts.
Elementary, middle/high	Work at a shelter or soup kitchen and write about the experience.
Elementary	Invite local businesses into the classroom while learning about professions and select one that needs a special project completed.
Other ideas?	

How can you integrate service learning into your student teaching practicum?

_____

_____

Why is it important to have students make the connection between learning information and service learning?

REFLECT

Three ways you may use to reflect on your practice during student teaching are listed on this page. Select the methods of reflection that will stimulate your thinking. Write in an *Inquiry Journal* during student teaching. This writing will serve as a data source for solving problems over time. Uncover your own assumptions, biases, and dispositions as you write in your journal several times each week.

✓ **Inquiry: Teacher Research as a Tool for Solving Classroom Problems and Enhancing Student Learning**

Select one issue that has emerged from the data in your journal. Has it challenged a belief or assumption you hold or verified something you have always believed? Summarize your thoughts and share with your supervisor.

_____

_____

_____

_____

Review the *Key Questions* in the PLAN section of this chapter. Which questions are still confusing? List them below and set up a time to discuss them with your cooperating teacher or supervisor.

_____

_____

_____

✓ **Self-Reflection: Analyze Your Teaching Strategies to Enhance Student Learning**

Select several tools from Chapter 3 and use them to guide your self-reflection. List the lessons you choose to analyze here. Use audio- and videotape to deepen your understanding of what is actually happening in your classroom. Share.

_____

_____

_____

_____

✓ **Critique: Feedback from Your Supervisor and Cooperating Teacher to Guide Your Planning, Instructional Practice, and Professionalism**

What type of feedback are you receiving related to your teaching strategies? How is this helpful to you? What do you need to do next to improve your practice?

_____

_____

_____

_____

Chapter 8

Assessing, Documenting, and Communicating Student Progress

How Do I Know What to Do?

Contact your students' parents. Don't wait to communicate bad news. In retrospect, I would have sent a postcard to each parent explaining who I was, including my email and phone. Throughout the practicum I would have sent postcards to parents indicating their child's strong and weak areas. Parental support is needed for student growth.

Student Teacher

Assessment is defined by Webster's dictionary as "to sit beside." *Evaluation,* on the other hand, is defined as "to examine and judge." Teachers find themselves in both roles as they informally may sit beside students and coach them to understand, or formally require students to take tests that are used for their final grade.

The purpose of assessment and evaluation is to increase student learning and understanding of the subject or skill. Sometimes students can pass the test but cannot explain the concept if they are asked to verbally share it. Does this mean the student has mastered the material or has just learned to pass a test that you have designed? If teaching for understanding and having students demonstrate what they have learned is the purpose of teaching, then assessing knowledge is critical. This means that lesson plans and teaching objectives need to match the assessment tools used throughout and at the end of the teaching unit. Also, if you allow students to use calculators for math activities during practice sessions, then calculators should be allowed for final assessment. Practice and learning objectives must be aligned with final assessment.

How do you know whether the student really understands what he has learned? Understanding can be demonstrated by observing the student explain, interpret, apply, persuade, create, design, defend, critique, correct, summarize, translate, compare, and contrast the information in his own words. Using Bloom's Taxonomy as a guide, you can create assessments, whether informal or formal, that specifically document what the students are doing to demonstrate their understanding of the material. Higher levels of thinking and understanding are represented by assessments that are more complex and authentic. For example, a test at level 1 (knowledge) could simply be a rote memorization of a list of vocabulary words, but a level-6 assessment would have to include more open-ended, complex thinking.

Teachers can use assessment tools to survey students using pretest forms and to gather information about what students already know about the subject being presented. They also use these same tools to discover what students don't know or are still confused about. Assessment tools assist teachers in making curriculum decisions and creating lesson plans that take students to the next level of learning.

Traditional assessments include the tests and quizzes with which all teachers are familiar. Alternative assessments are nontraditional and offer a variety of approaches that allow students to demonstrate their understanding by showing what they know. These alternative assessments include student portfolios, open-ended questions, and performance. During your student teaching, you should try multiple assessment strategies to gain insight into the level of understanding your students hold.

Your assessment tools should be clearly matched to standards you are striving for in your classroom. Make sure the activities you design in your lessons actually relate to what you want the students to learn! Sometimes students do poorly on a test and when the teacher reviews the test he discovers it did not relate to objective taught!

There are a wide variety of assessments available to you as a student teacher. Do not limit yourself to traditional paper-and-pencil tests and quizzes. Review the alternative paper-and-pencil approaches in this chapter to give your students a variety of options for measuring success. Keep in mind the diverse learning styles of your students. Review your instructional strategies in the previous chapter and design measures that match!

Finally, don't forget to tell your students how you will be assessing their progress *before* you begin the lesson. Also create opportunities for your students be part of both peer and self-assessment whenever possible. Evaluating your students' progress is the most important part of teaching. It lets you know what to do next, where to modify your instruction, and what students need to know and be able to do.

This chapter serves as an overview and reminder of the assessment, documentation, and communication strategies you have learned in your teaching methods courses. If you need more information about assessment, use the CONNECT page in this chapter to assist you.

Discussing Professional Standards

QUALITY CONVERSATIONS TO ENHANCE STUDENT LEARNING

National standards guide new teacher preparation in the United States. The INTASC created 10 principles for effective teaching. These principles are offered to you as a way to focus your attention on these key elements of practice. The "bottom line" is all about student learning. Are your students learning? How do you know?

Use these pages in each chapter to frame a quality conversation with your cooperating teacher and university supervisor. Don't be afraid to ask your own questions, too. Also use the REFLECT pages at the end of each chapter to deepen your thinking and to continue your quality conversations throughout the practium experience and into your first year of teaching.

INTASC Principles

Focus for Chapter 8

Discuss:

Principle #8   The teacher understands and uses formal and informal assessment strategies to evaluate and ensure the continuous intellectual, social, and physical development of the learner.

Review:

Principle #10   The teacher fosters relationships with school colleagues, parents, and agencies in the larger community to support students' learning and well-being.

ASK YOURSELF   What do these principles mean to me right now? How will I know if I have achieved these principles?

DISCUSS WITH YOUR SUPERVISOR OR COOPERATING TEACHER

How will your supervisor/cooperating teacher know if you have achieved these principles? What evidence will you have to demonstrate these skills to them?

How will you know if your students have learned as a result of your teaching?

PLAN

USE ADVICE FROM FORMER STUDENT TEACHERS

Talk to student teachers who have just completed the experience and review the tips below to guide you.

- Let your students assess their own progress! Compare their measures to your own.
- Remember that each student is someone's child. Put yourself in that parent's position every time you call home or conduct a parent-teacher meeting.
- Keep your eyes open and observe student growth in informal ways. Assessment is an ongoing skill for a teacher. It does not just happen at test time.

PROCESS YOUR EXPERIENCE

Respond to the Key Questions below by completing the process pages in each chapter. These ACTs will encourage you to deepen your thinking about teaching and learning. Write on the pages and save them to review at the end of the experience.

KEY QUESTIONS

1. How do I assess and evaluate student progress in my classroom?

2. How do I record and document student progress?

3. How do I communicate progress to students and parents?

PLAN

TAKE CARE OF YOURSELF AND AVOID STRESS

Plan to avoid the typical stresses of student teaching by following advice from cooperating teachers and university supervisors.

THINK OF OTHERS!

When you take the time to thank someone or send a note of appreciation, your worries and stresses seem lessened.

- Phone calls to parents about their child's progress are wonderful ways to make the parents feel good, and the students you call always hear about it!
- Don't forget to thank your cooperating teacher from time to time. She is putting in extra time that you may not realize, and having another "teacher" in the classroom all day long can be tedious.

It is surprising how *you* will feel after you recognize all the *good* that is going on around you, and when you thank others it comes back to you!

Who will you compliment this week?

PLAN YOUR WEEK

Priority List

Done	Tasks	Priority	Complete by When?

Place things to do on the day you would like to do them.

Monday Date:	Tuesday Date:	Wednesday Date:	Thursday Date:	Friday Date:

CONNECT

CONNECT is a resource page with ideas and suggestions to support you during student teaching. Select and complete any CONNECT items that will enhance your experience in the classroom.

CONNECT with people

- Parents
  Talk with parents of your students to ask how they see "progress" with their children. Set up a regularly scheduled "phone home" contact plan in which you call each student's home at least once a month.
- Teachers
  Talk with teachers who worked with students in previous grades to measure progress over time.

CONNECT with readings & resources

- Books and authors to explore on the Internet or at your local library
  Assessing Bilingual Children, K–3 by Stefanakis (Heinemann)
  Assessment Is Instruction by Glazer (Christopher-Gordon)
  Assessment Alternatives for Diverse Classrooms by Farr and Trumbull (Christopher-Gordon)
  Communication for the Classroom Teacher by Cooper and Simonds (Allyn and Bacon)
  Assessment & Instruction of Culturally & Linguistically Diverse Students with or At-Risk of Learning Problems by Gonzalez, Brusca-Vega, and Yawkey (Allyn and Bacon)

CONNECT technology to teaching

- Visit this website:
  http://www.relearning.org for assessment tools
- Teacher software and much more = http://www.teachervision.com
- Read to integrate technology into your classroom
  The Technological Classroom by Heide (Christopher-Gordon)
  The Integrated Technology Classroom by Riedl (Allyn and Bacon)

ACT
Process 8.1   Standards—How Are Students Evaluated?

Review all tests that the students in your class will be required to take this year to gain some understanding of the context in which you are working. Some students in high school may be taking SATs for college or performance tests for admission into trade or art schools. Elementary students may be taking basic skills tests and preschool students may be taking readiness skill tests to show where they are developmentally.

All these tests relate to the environment for learning you are attempting to create with your students in your cooperating teacher's classroom. A *high-stakes test* is defined as one that has a consequence for failure. For example, if you fail the high school exit test, you don't graduate, or if you don't attain a certain score on the SAT, you don't get into certain colleges.

STATE TESTING INITIATIVES
What is the purpose of the program?

Does the state have a statewide testing program?

Are the students required to pass a high school exit exam? When is it given? What is the test?

Are there other state tests required? Which grade levels? Ask to review a copy of the tests if they are at your grade level.

What standards or frameworks are the tests based on? How will this state test affect the curriculum you teach in your classroom?

DISTRICT TESTING PROGRAM
What is the purpose of these tests?

Does the district require tests for certain grades? Note the test names:

_____

Are these tests similar to the state tests? How?

CLASSROOM ASSESSMENT AND EVALUATION PROCEDURES

How does your cooperating teacher use *informal* assessment for "sit beside" learning?

How does your cooperating teacher *formally* assess students for understanding?

ACT
Process 8.2 Classroom Assessment— A Developmental Continuum

FORMATIVE ASSESSMENT IS PRACTICE—YOUR DRESS REHEARSAL

It is authentic, ongoing, sit beside, self-assessing, learn as we go, practice, group work, conversations, checklists, surveys, drill, practice tests.

When would you use formative assessments in teaching? List your ideas here.

SUMMATIVE ASSESSMENT IS FINAL—THE OPENING NIGHT OF THE PLAY

It is the final test, grade given to an individual student, final evaluation, judgment given at the end of the unit or term, report card grade, SAT final product, paper test, project artwork, final performance, Spanish oral exam.

When would you use summative evaluation? List your ideas here.

ACT
Process 8.3 Linking My Lesson Plan to
My Assessment Instrument

Lesson planning and assessment are linked. Your lesson plan and your assessment or evaluation of the lesson should be written at the same time. This ensures that your students will be responding to the key questions and objectives you established. What do you want students to be able to do?

Review a lesson plan you recently created. Were your objectives clear? Do you know what you wanted students to learn? What type of assessment did you create or do you need to create to measure student achievement? Did your assessment approach match your lesson's activities?

How does your cooperating teacher create forms of assessment? How do the forms relate to the lesson plan and lesson taught?

How do you know when students have developed an understanding of a skill or topic?

ACT
Process 8.4   Tapping into Students' Prior Knowledge

An important aspect of assessment is knowing where students are before you begin teaching. Students come to your classroom with varied backgrounds and experience levels related to the topic you may be presenting. Being able to "assess" this knowledge as part of your regular planning process is important to designing lessons that meet the needs of the diverse learners in your classroom.

1. How have you experienced teachers tapping into your prior knowledge?

2. How have you observed your cooperating teacher tapping into your students' prior knowledge?

Ways to tap in...
- Ask students privately on paper before the lesson begins...
  What do you already know about this topic/skill?
  What do you think you know or have you heard about this topic/skill?
  What would you like to learn or know?
- Collect the papers, and at the end of the unit or lesson ask students what they learned and have them write it on the bottom of the sheet they had previously started.
- Give a pretest on the topic, testing for spelling words, math skill, and so on.
- Have students write a paragraph about what they know about the topic.

Tapping in can avoid teaching students who may already *know* the information. It also assists you in designing lessons to meet the current needs of your students.

Tapping in can also serve as a check-in toward the middle and near the end of the term to let you know how closely the lesson objectives are being met.

ACT
Process 8.5 How Do Teachers Measure Student Learning?
Product or Process?

How do you observe student achievement? Will a product let you know that the student achieved the objectives or do you need to observe the student perform and demonstrate the skill or understanding of the topic?

Your assessment/evaluation depends on the lesson's objective. Be sure the achievement measure you require matches the objective you designed in your lesson plan.

Product (paper/pencil)	*Product (visual)*	*Performance Process (with or without product)*
Essay	Poster	Oral report
Book report	Banner	Speech
Biography	Model	Rap
Journal	Diagram	Dramatization
Letter	Display	Debate
Editorial	Videotape or audiotape	Song
Script	Portfolio	Poem
Test	Exhibit	Demonstration
Research report	Painting	Interview
Short answers	Photo	Skit
Position paper	Website	News report

Are your lessons always requiring the same type of assessment or evaluation? Are you providing alternative assessments for all learners?

Assessments and evaluations should include a combination of

- **Traditional**
  Teacher-made or standardized tests that have only one right answer
  Norm- or criterion-referenced tests
  Knowledge and comprehension levels of Bloom's Taxonomy
  Individual's prior knowledge of objectives through pretesting

- **Open-Ended**
  Guided questions
  Multistep problems
  Higher levels of Bloom's Taxonomy
  Problem-solving approach to thinking

- **Performance**
  Hands-on projects and demonstration of skills and understanding
  More than one right answer
  Portfolios
  Creative problem solving through the arts

- **Informal**
  Observation of students in groups or individually

How are the students in your classroom being evaluated or assessed informally?

What are the assessment instruments your cooperating teacher is using?

ACT
Process 8.6　What Should Students Know and Be Able to Do?

Interview your cooperating teacher about the classroom standards and expectations for all learners in the classroom.

What **SOME** Students Need to Know and Be Able to Do	How are these students selected? What is the knowledge they will "go beyond" in the classroom. How will they get the information? How will you know they achieved beyond?
What **MOST** Students Need to Know and Be Able to Do	Who are these students? How did you select the information they need to know?
What **ALL** Students Need to Know and Be Able to Do	Minimum Standard: "Passing" for ALL students. How is this determined?

Use this information to design your lesson plans, select appropriate instructional strategies, and assess progress.

Sample Rubric for Writing Assignment

5	**Demonstrates High Skill** Well organized and clear; few grammatical errors; appropriate for level; exceeds standards
4	**Clearly Demonstrates Skill** Loosely organized but main ideas; some errors; most writing appropriate; meets standards
3	**Demonstrates Progress** Some attempt to include main ideas; many errors but some clarity; partial answer; meets some standards
2	**Requires Intervention** Lack of organization; lack of clarity; full of errors; does not meet standards sufficiently
1	**Unsatisfactory** Incomplete; does not meet standards; inapropriate response

Create Your Own Rubric for a Lesson You Will Be Teaching

5	**Demonstrates High Skill**
4	**Clearly Demonstrates Skill**
3	**Demonstrates Progress**
2	**Requires Intervention**
1	**Unsatisfactory**

ACT
Process 8.8   Portfolio Assessment

A *portfolio* is a collection of student work that represents growth over time. Writing portfolios may include drafts as well as final copies of writing over a term or a school year. One important aspect of a portfolio is the student's reflection about why she selected a piece for the portfolio or what she learned by completing a certain task. If this process is omitted, then the portfolio just serves as a "folder" of student work.

Some teachers require certain documents that must be part of the portfolio, whereas others allow students to select them. A combination of both is often helpful in determining student progress. A rubric for assessing the value of the portfolio is necessary if you want to measure how effectively students collected and reflected on the work inside.

Portfolios are often difficult to manage and oversee in a busy teacher's classroom. However, they do measure skills that traditional paper-and-pencil assessments cannot do. They also require students to use their multiple intelligence skills as well as higher-order thinking in Bloom's Taxonomy. All students may not want to or need to develop a portfolio, but it is an excellent option in a differentiated instruction classroom.

How is your cooperating teacher using portfolios?

How is the portfolio assessed?

How does this assessment relate to state standards?

ELECTRONIC PORTFOLIOS AND WEBPAGES

More classrooms now have computers, and electronic portfolios are becoming more popular as vehicles for documenting student progress.

Explore the possibility of using a website or e-portfolio in your classroom!

ACT
Process 8.9   Authentic Assessment

Authentic is defined as an alternative approach to observing student achievement. It allows the teacher to see whether the student can explain, demonstrate, and justify the skill or understanding in his own words, revealing understanding of the concepts, objectives, and key questions. Authentic assessments are useful with all students, but particularly helpful with children with special needs, bilingual students, and gifted and talented students who may not be able to respond to summative tests.

Where are the students in your classroom right now? What do they already know?

HOW TO FIND OUT:

Survey
Use teacher-made pretest
Tap into prior knowledge
Review student file
Talk with parents
Check reading level

1. Do any of the students have special needs? Emotional or physical?

_____

_____

_____

How will you assess their progress and achievement?

_____

_____

_____

2. Are any of the students second language/bilingual?

_____

_____

_____

How will you plan accordingly to assess and evaluate their progress?

_____

_____

_____

ACT
Process 8.10   Record-Keeping Strategies

Teachers use a variety of systems to keep track of student progress. A common way is to use a grade book. However, many teachers use different systems within their grade books. Ask your cooperating teacher to share his system with you.

COOPERATING TEACHER'S GRADEBOOK SYSTEM

_____

_____

_____

In addition to using grade books, teachers may make anecdotal comments and use journals, index file boxes, or their own plan books to keep track. Other teachers use checklists or progress charts. Document three other ways to record information and why a teacher might use these systems in addition to a grade book.

_____

_____

_____

How do you decide whether a record-keeping system is effective?

_____ When reviewing a strategy, ask: **Is it easy to use?** (Is it something I will use?)

_____ Ask: **Is it easy to read?** (Can I scan it quickly for information?)

_____ Ask: **Can I derive patterns from it?** (Over time do I see student progress?)

_____ Use a highlighter to mark the holes in your grade book to scan for missing grades easily.

_____ Use another color highlighter for any grade below average to scan problem areas quickly.

Interview other teachers to see how they document their students' progress. List their ideas here.

ACT
Process 8.11   Sample Grade Book

Use this format or create one of your own to record student progress.

Name	Grade Date	Grade Date	Grade Date	Grade Date	Grade Date	Grade Date

ACT
Process 8.12 Group and Self-Evaluation
How Can Students Monitor Their Own Progress?

Does your cooperating teacher use any student self-assessment tools? Does she ask students to assess their own learning? If so, how? Examples here illustrate ways individuals and groups can assess their own progress.

INDIVIDUAL ASSESSMENT OF DAILY WORK

Hard or Easy?
- Ask students whether they are finding the work hard or easy.
- Make a graph to see how many students are finding things hard or easy.

What Are You Learning?
- Take a minute at the end of each class as part of your closing to ask students to write two things they learned in class today.
- Collect and review to see how you did as a teacher in presenting your objectives. This exercise can serve two purposes: (1) to see what they recall and (2) to let you know how to plan the next lesson.

More Time?
- Have students vote whether they think they need more time on the concept.
- Let students reply anonymously on paper or by putting their heads down and raising their hands.
- Write your own prediction of how the lesson went and what they will say before reading the students' responses.

Work Habits
Create a worksheet that asks questions that the students have to rate from 1 to 5. For example:
- I worked hard in groups today
- I understand the concepts presented.

Teacher Assessment
Create a sheet about you and your skills in teaching. Rate each 1 to 5. For example:
- My teacher presents information in a way I can understand.
- My teacher listens to my questions.
- There is time in class for me to practice the skill.

GROUP ASSESSMENT OF DAILY WORK

Create a sheet for cooperating groups to assess their ability to work together and learn the information in a group. They have to come to consensus in their rating of each item you create.

Sample questions for a cooperative group assessment form:

1. How did you contribute to the group work today?

2. What did each member of the group do to contribute to your learning?

3. How would you grade your group today: excellent   very good   good   fair   poor
   Why?

4. What grade would you give yourself?   excellent   very good   good   fair   poor
   Why?

5. What did you like most about working in this group?

6. What would you do differently next time you are working in a group?

7. Is there anything else the teacher needs to know?

ACT
Process 8.13   Communicating with Students

Teachers use a variety of systems to communicate with their students and keep them on track. The most common formats are the progress slip and the report card, which both go home to parents (see ACT Process 8.14). Many teachers show these to students first, before they are sent home. Remember that progress may include growth in behavior as well as academics.

In addition to these traditional approaches, teachers are using other procedures to directly communicate with students. Ask your cooperating teacher to share samples/ideas of any of the following communication systems she is familiar with or has used.

_____ 1. **Student mailboxes/Teacher mailbox.** Teachers and students can leave notes for one another about assignments, papers due, make-up work, etc.

_____ 2. **Student conference.** Teacher establishes a schedule and meets with individual students privately about progress. All students meet with teacher, not just failing students.

_____ 3. **Progress chart.** A subject-related progress chart is given to each student that visually documents the number of assignments completed, scores, projects, etc.

_____ 4. **Warnings.** When in danger of failing, a student receives a "red" note.

_____ 5. **Compliments.** Written or verbal acknowledgment of quality work.

_____ 6. **Checklist.** Placed inside daily or weekly folders—students can see what has been checked by you and approved for credit.

_____ 7. **Progress list.** Secondary students may be instructed to maintain their own grades.

_____ 8. **Midterm progress reports.** These list completed assignments and suggestions for improvement.

_____ 9. **Student-led parent conference.** When students attend and share their progress with the parents.

Other ideas:

ACT
Process 8.14   Communicating with Parents and Guardians

Teachers communicate with parents for many reasons, including how their child interacts with other students, how the child's behavior is in class, and/or what the academic progress of the student is at the time of the conversation. Student teachers need to be aware of the variety of ways to communicate this information.

Some common procedures include:

____ 1. **Telephone call conferences** (Suggestion: Send a note home telling parents what time you will be calling.)
   - To compliment students
   - To give warnings

____ 2. **Written**
   - Informal notes to parents
   - Formal progress slips from school office/midterm reports
   - Formal progress slips/behavior checklists—teacher designed
   - Daily homework sheets initialed by teacher and sent home

____ 3. **Meetings**
   - Informal
   - Regarding a particular issue
   - Formal—regular basis for a particular student, including other teachers, principal, guidance, etc.
   - Parent conference—appointments for parents on a certain day with or without students

____ 4. **Report cards**
   - Delivered by students
   - Picked up by parents

____ 5. **Group meetings with parents**
   - Open house evening with or without students
   - Special event in your classroom

Ask your cooperating teacher how he communicates with parents. List ideas here.

REFLECT

Three ways you may use to reflect on your practice during student teaching are listed on this page. Select the methods of reflection that will stimulate your thinking. Write in an *Inquiry Journal* during student teaching. This writing will serve as a data source for solving problems over time. Uncover your own assumptions, biases, and dispositions as you write in your journal several times each week.

✓ **Inquiry: Teacher Research as a Tool for Solving Classroom Problems and Enhancing Student Learning**

List the questions you have about assessment and student learning. Select one and create a research question that will identify the issue. Observe and collect data to find out more about this issue. If the question relates to one student not learning, create an intervention (or use a new strategy) to assist the learning and write about what happens as a result.

_____

_____

_____

Review the *Key Questions* in the PLAN section of this chapter. Which questions are still confusing? List them below and set up a time to discuss them with your cooperating teacher or supervisor.

_____

_____

_____

✓ **Self-Reflection: Analyze Your Teaching Strategies to Enhance Student Learning** (*Use the processes in Chapter 3 to guide your self-reflection.*)

How do you know your students are learning? How are you teaching for understanding? Do you think students know what the "purpose" of each lesson is?

_____

_____

What are you learning about yourself as a teacher through this self-reflection process?

_____

_____

✓ **Critique: Feedback from Your Supervisor and Cooperating Teacher to Guide Your Planning, Instructional Practice, and Professionalism**

Answer this question: How am I using the feedback from others to improve student learning in my lessons?

_____

_____

_____

Chapter 9

Completing the Practicum Experience

What Needs to Be Done?

Congratulations! You have just completed one of the most serious and challenging experiences of your college career.

Student Teacher

As you complete your student teaching experience, you should feel a sense of satisfaction. You have participated in an intense experience that has prepared you to become a teacher. Whether you completed a full semester or a whole school year, you have had the opportunity to be in a classroom in the role of the teacher.

Review all the REFLECTs and CONNECTs you wrote throughout the semester. How have you grown and changed in this short time? How have these new relationships affected you as a teacher and as a person? What has this experience given you that you will bring to your own classroom?

Take time to acknowledge the people and the students who have worked with you as you developed your teaching skills. Elaborate gifts are not expected. Simple handwritten thank-you notes with your appreciative comments mean the most to teachers. How will you leave this school and the students?

As you complete this practicum course, two important summative actions must be taken at the end of the semester:

1. *A Grade Submitted for Your Transcript.* Grading procedures vary. Be sure you are clear on how on your grade is being determined. If self-evaluation is a component of grading, be sure to complete your self-evaluation and submit it on time. Typically, the university supervisor submits the grade after gaining input from the cooperating teacher. Remember, the grade includes *all* requirements that needed to be completed during this time, such as your journal and student teaching binder.

2. *Recommendation for Teacher Certification.* A certificate of teaching is a license that will be sent to you after you formally apply to the state. Procedures vary from state to state, so you need to work closely with your college certification officer and Field Office or Office of Practicum Experiences to follow your

state's procedures. If your college program has been officially "approved" by the state, you will receive an endorsement, usually placed on your transcript. Your cooperating teacher may also be asked to write a letter of recommendation for certification as well as signing other state forms.

This is not the end of your teaching experience. Completion leads to new beginnings, and by completing student teaching you are *opening the door to the teaching profession*. Complete the activities in this chapter and look forward to the next section, which will guide you through the *new door* by assisting you in the job search and settling you into your new classroom.

Discussing Professional Standards

QUALITY CONVERSATIONS TO ENHANCE STUDENT LEARNING

National standards guide new teacher preparation in the United States. The INTASC created 10 principles for effective teaching. These principles are offered to you as a way to focus your attention on these key elements of practice. The "bottom line" is all about student learning. Are your students learning? How do you know?

Use these pages in each chapter to frame a quality conversation with your cooperating teacher and university supervisor. Don't be afraid to ask your own questions, too. Also use the REFLECT pages at the end of each chapter to deepen your thinking and to continue your quality conversations throughout the practium experience and into your first year of teaching.

INTASC Principles

Focus for Chapter 9

Review:
All Principles 1–10

Principle #9 The teacher is a reflective practitioner who continually evaluates the effects of his or her choices and actions of others (students, parents, and other professionals in the learning community) and who actively seeks out opportunities to grow professionally.

ASK YOURSELF What do these principles mean to me right now? How will I know if I have achieved these principles?

DISCUSS WITH YOUR SUPERVISOR OR COOPERATING TEACHER

How will your supervisor/cooperating teacher know if you have achieved these principles? What evidence will you have to demonstrate these skills to them?

How will you know if your students have learned as a result of your teaching?

PLAN

USE ADVICE FROM FORMER STUDENT TEACHERS

Talk to student teachers who have just completed the experience and review the tips below to guide you.

- Remember that you don't have to be perfect at the end of student teaching. In fact, this is just the beginning of your developmental process. Acknowledge your personal and professional growth! Celebrate!
- Invite your students to give you feedback. Create an easy survey you can give them and review their answers carefully.
- Take some time to process all of the feedback you have been given and write your own self-evaluation. Compare your comments with others.

PROCESS YOUR EXPERIENCE

Respond to the Key Questions below by completing the process pages in each chapter. These ACTs will encourage you to deepen your thinking about teaching and learning. Write on the pages and save them to review at the end of the experience.

KEY QUESTIONS

1. How does the end of student teaching compare to my first week?

2. How do I say good-bye and thank you?

3. What will the college evaluation consist of?

4. How will the cooperating teacher recommend me for certification?

5. How do I apply for certification?

6. How do I evaluate this experience?

7. How would I advise future student teachers?

PLAN

TAKE CARE OF YOURSELF AND AVOID STRESS

Plan to avoid the typical stresses of student teaching by following advice from cooperating teachers and university supervisors.

ACKNOWLEDGE THE SUCCESSFUL MOMENTS!

Treasure the successful moments with students you have worked with during this semester. Recall the class periods when everything "clicked" and the lesson went on without a hitch; you didn't run out of time or have too much time left over. Think of the time a student reached out for help or advice and you were there, and the time when the cooperating teacher said it was all coming together.

What are some of your treasured moments this semester?

PLAN YOUR WEEK

Priority List

Done	Tasks	Priority	Complete by When?

Place things to do on the day you would like to do them.

Monday Date:	Tuesday Date:	Wednesday Date:	Thursday Date:	Friday Date:

CONNECT

CONNECT is a resource page with ideas and suggestions to support you during student teaching. Select and complete any CONNECT items that will enhance your experience in the classroom.

CONNECT with people

- Favorite people
  Acknowledge personally all the people who helped you through the semester. It does "take a village" to educate students, and you had the opportunity to work with many of them. Ask them for final thoughts and advice.

- Cooperating teacher
  What do you need to talk about that you haven't already taken time for? Take the time now or set up a time when student teaching is over to reconnect.

CONNECT with readings & resources

- Books and authors to explore on the Internet or at your local library
  Mentors, Masters, and Mrs. MacGregor compiled by Bluestein (Health Communications, Deerfield Beach, Florida)
  Teacher Therapy by Katafiasz (Abbey Press)
  Tips from the Trenches: America's Best Teachers Describe Effective Classroom Methods by Chase and Chase (Technomic Publications)
  Dear Teacher: Daily Affirmations for Teachers Who Inspire by Witham (Brownlow)

CONNECT technology to teaching

- Check out this website:
  Education Station includes ways to integrate technology into the classroom with on-line programs, projects, and lesson plans.
  http://www.csun.edu/~vceed009/

- If you missed this book in Chapter 1, read
  World Wide Web for Teachers by Cafolla et al. (Allyn and Bacon)

ACT
Process 9.1   How Have I Changed?

You made it! Do you remember reading the quote at the beginning of Chapter 1? *"Don't blink; it will be over before you know it!"*—well it is over!

How have you changed?

Review your original assumptions about teaching and learning (ACT Process 1.9). How are they different? The same? What have you learned?

What is your current attitude/disposition about teaching and becoming a teacher?

Review the goals you wrote (ACT Process 1.4). Did you reach them? Did they change along the way? If so, why?

Reread all your inquiry journals. What stands out for you as "change" in your attitude, goals, perceptions, ideas, and so on?

What is the single-most important thing you have learned from this experience?

Do you plan to teach as a professional career choice? Why? Why not?

If you are planning to teach, read the next three chapters to guide you into the professional job search as well as into your first classroom. GOOD LUCK!

ACT
Process 9.2   Student Teaching Portfolio Final Checklist

If your portfolio is required, you should obtain a copy of the university guidelines for assessing it. If your portfolio is not required as a summation of your college practicum and you are completing it for the job interview and for future use, follow the suggestions below to assess you own work.

SELF-ASSESSMENT

Use the self-assessment of your portfolio as an activity that encourages you to look at what you found most difficult about creating the portfolio.

Ask yourself:

> How does this portfolio represent my growth as a teacher?
> Where did I grow the most?
> Where do I still need to focus my efforts?

PEER ASSESSMENT

Use the portfolio to gain feedback about your teacher portfolio.

Ask other student teachers:

> What did you like about my teacher portfolio?
> What do you see is "missing"?
> Do you have a compliment for me?

Read someone else's portfolio and answer the same questions for them.

COOPERATING TEACHER AND UNIVERSITY SUPERVISOR FEEDBACK

Invite your support team to give you suggestions before you completely finish your portfolio.

Ask them:

> How can I improve my portfolio?
> What do you like about my portfolio?

ACT
Process 9.3   Good-Bye and Thank You!

As part of your completion, you must acknowledge those who assisted you through this exhilarating and sometimes stressful experience. Think about the ways you interacted with these people and write a short, personal note or letter thanking them. Personal memories or stories that will remain with you forever are important to share.

People to thank with a short, personal note or poem:

____ Cooperating teacher

____ Students—a group letter or poem

____ Other people in the building who have helped, such as teacher aides, department chair, secretary (see important people list in Chapter 2)

SAMPLE LETTER FOR ELEMENTARY STUDENTS

Dear Room ____,

Saying good-bye is never easy. It has been hard for me to think about leaving your classroom. From the first moment I met all of you I knew this was going to be a positive experience.

I am giving you a plant for the classroom because both you and I have done a lot of growing this term. I have learned so many wonderful things from your teacher and from each of you that I will bring to my own classroom. I will always hold a special place in my memories for this class. Be good, study hard, and take care of this plant and watch it grow!

Sincerely,

Ms./Mr. _____

In addition to your personal note, a small gift may be appropriate for either the cooperating teacher or the classroom.

_____ A book that you have signed with date and year for the school or class library

_____ A plant for the classroom

_____ A bouquet of flowers

_____ A cake in a special shape or decorated in a theme of a unit you taught

_____ A special unit that you developed that you copy and leave with the teacher

_____ A collection of the students' writings put together in a book format

_____ Special supplies for the classroom

_____ Photographs displayed in a poster or scrapbook

_____ A gift certificate

_____ An audiotaped message from you

_____ A classroom video that you made with them

_____ Other

_____ Other

ACT
Process 9.4   Final Evaluation—The Supervisor's
Summative Report
Four Steps to the Final Grade

STEP ONE: COMPLETION OF REQUIREMENTS

Review the syllabus requirements and check for completion.

Did I do everything I was asked to do?

_____ Text and readings

_____ Observation forms

_____ Products that need to be complete (e.g., samples of lesson plans, unit, teaching binder)

_____ College-related requirements (e.g., attendance on campus for seminar or other required events)

_____ Journal with weekly entry

_____ Other requirements _____

_____ List any extra credit completed during the semester and include it in your teaching binder

Did I complete all requirements on time and present them clearly and free of error?

STEP TWO: COMPETENCE IN FIELD EXPERIENCE
AND RELATED REQUIREMENTS

Review your field experience for evidence of competence.

Review the criteria for outstanding student teacher and the rubric from Chapter 3.

Ask yourself: How do I match up with the criteria?

_____ Subject matter knowledge

_____ Communication

_____ Instructional practice

_____ Evaluation

_____ Problem solving

_____ Equity

_____ Professionalism

Review all forms completed throughout the semester:

_____ Initial visit

_____ Midterm

_____ Final observation

_____ Other informal verbal feedback you noted

_____ Other written feedback

Review your journal entries, audiotapes, and videotapes.

Did I demonstrate a beginning level of competence in all areas?

STEP THREE: DOCUMENTING SCHOOL OF EDUCATION THEMES

Was I required to demonstrate evidence of the School of Education themes?

Sample themes:
   Promoting social justice
   Constructing knowledge
   Inquiring into practice
   Accommodating diversity
   Collaborating with others

Where did I demonstrate them? How would my supervisor know?

Before meeting with your supervisor and after you have reviewed all materials, ask yourself what you think your final grade will be based on

- Your self-assessment of completion and competency
- Feedback you have received throughout the semester

STEP FOUR: COMPARE YOUR SELF-ASSESSMENT WITH THAT OF UNIVERSITY SUPERVISOR

Meet with your college supervisor at your close-out meeting and compare your self-assessment with the evaluation the supervisor has prepared. Be sure to bring all completed requirements and your student teaching binder for final review. The supervisor will now be ready to complete the summative report.

Typically, grades are assigned by college supervisors with input from cooperating teachers. This is done at a meeting or through a phone call near the end of the semester. Because there are many college requirements, the supervisor must take responsibility for compiling all information and recommending the final grade. Final grades for student teachers are then submitted to the Director of Practicum or Field Experiences and forwarded to the registrar for placement on the transcript.

The final summative report consists of the grade and a short narrative to support the grade. The narrative usually uses the certification competencies as a format.

OPTIONAL JOB RECOMMENDATION LETTER

Student teachers often ask supervisors to write letters of recommendation for the job search. If you feel your final summative report is acceptable, this may be used as part of your teacher portfolio for the job search. If you require another format, give your supervisor ample notice.

ACT
Process 9.5 Cooperating Teacher Recommendation
for License

As part of some state certification procedures, the cooperating teacher is often required to write a letter of recommendation stating your competence as a beginning teacher. You may want to also use this letter for your teacher portfolio for the job search.

This letter could consist of...

- The statement that you are recommended for state _____ certification
- An example(s) of work you have done that demonstrates your competencies
- The date and semester you student taught
- A brief description of the school and type of classroom(s) in which you worked
- Why your cooperating teacher thinks you would be a good teacher

What would you like your cooperating teacher to include in your sample letter?

List your ideas here

_____
_____
_____
_____
_____
_____
_____
_____
_____
_____
_____
_____
_____
_____

Share these ideas and a copy of your résumé and student teaching profile with your cooperating teacher to assist her in writing your final recommendation.

ACT
Process 9.6 Application for State Teacher License

You will apply for state certification or license in the state in which you complete student teaching. This certification can then be fairly easily transferred to other states in the United States. Check the certification procedures in your teacher education program to ensure a smooth application process.

LICENSURE WHERE YOU COMPLETED STUDENT TEACHING

☐ Complete all final paperwork with your university supervisor and receive your grade.

☐ Meet with the university certification officer to follow school procedures.

☐ Complete application and mail to State Department of Certification.

☐ Register for and successfully pass any state teacher test mandated for certification.

OUT-OF-STATE TEACHING LICENSE

☐ Review an reciprocity procedure. *Reciprocity* means that your college preparation is acceptable to another state and is considered to be comparable. It does not mean you are "automatically" certified in another state, nor does it mean you won't have any additional requirements for that state.

☐ Request an application and verification of completion of student teaching. Usually, the state will send you a form that needs to be completed by your college certification officer indicating that you completed an "approved program" in that state. This verification form is used to begin your application for certification in that state. You may also need to take a course or a teacher test if that state requires either. Note: When mailing forms to the certification officer, the process is usually speeded up by also enclosing a copy of your transcript and evidence of student teaching (practicum/clinical report).

☐ Contact the state to which you are applying and ask about current regulations.

Note what you need to check on regarding certification:

_____

_____

ACT
Process 9.7   Final Self-Evaluation

As you complete the experience, you can assist future student teachers and the Office of Practicum Experiences by

1. Updating the school profile.

   Any new information from the school about curriculum

   New hours for the school

   New principal

   Other?

2. Updating the cooperating teacher's profile.

   If you use this school regularly, a profile of the cooperating teacher's classroom can assist others in having an understanding of this teacher's style. Ask if there is a form for this.

3. Writing your personal comments about your student teaching experience.

   Information about the placement process

   The cooperating teacher

   The field requirements

   The university supervisor

Write your comments on any formal evaluation that is available to you or write a letter to the director giving your input.

It is appropriate to give suggestions on ways in which the program can be approved and also to give compliments on ways in which the program is strong.

What will you highlight in your evaluation?

_____

_____

_____

_____

ACT
Process 9.8   Advice for Future Student Teachers

Prepare an open letter to students who may be in pre-practicum experiences now or who are preparing for their full practicum experiences. Write neatly or type so that your letter can be copied and shared or placed in a binder for prospective students to read. Student teachers listen to other student teachers. Share what you have learned. Include some lesson plans or articles that you read this semester that you saved in your own student teaching binder. This letter is a way of leaving a legacy to future teachers.

DRAFT SAMPLE LETTER

Date: _____

Dear Future Student Teacher,

I have just completed my full practicum experience, and I have some advice for you as you begin preparing yourself for your student teaching next semester.

_____

_____

_____

_____

_____

_____

_____

I have also attached two of my favorite lesson plans and an article that I found to be helpful.

Sincerely,

Student Teacher

Grade Level

If you are willing to talk to prospective student teachers, leave your E-mail or phone number so you can be contacted.

ACT
Process 9.9 Public Portfolio Sharing

General guidelines: Do not feel you have to share every single page! You may want to give your portfolio to another person to have him look through it at his own pace. The suggestions below are ways to verbally share your work.

PAIRED SHARE: SHARING WITH ANOTHER STUDENT TEACHER

- Highlight two areas of the portfolio where you feel you learned the most.
- Show your pictures.
- Select ONE successful lesson and share why it was successful.
- Ask your partner ONE question after he or she has shared!

SHARING WITH A SMALL GROUP

- Each person goes around the group and shares ONE aspect of the portfolio of which she is most proud (i.e., a lesson she taught, an observation, etc.)
- Everyone in the group gets to ask another person ONE question about his or her portfolio.
- Everyone holds up ONE photo at the same time and everyone looks at them to see what is there and why they chose that one.

SHARING WITH A PANEL OF SUPERVISORS AND/OR COOPERATING TEACHERS

- Follow any guidelines the panel has suggested.
- Share the school, social context, and so on.
- Share what you learned about teaching, using examples from your portfolio.
- Share how you changed from beginning to now.

Be sure to share your portfolio with someone! You have done lots of work and it is important to be acknowledged! Save this and learn how to re-create it as an interview portfolio in the next chapter.

REFLECT

Three ways you may use to reflect on your practice during student teaching are listed on this page. Select the methods of reflection that will stimulate your thinking. Write in an *Inquiry Journal* during student teaching. This writing will serve as a data source for solving problems over time. Uncover your own assumptions, biases, and dispositions as you write in your journal several times each week.

✓ **Inquiry: Teacher Research as a Tool for Solving Classroom Problems and Enhancing Student Learning**

Reread all of your inquiry journal entries for the semester (or year). What do you notice? What themes are emerging from your own observations and inquiry into practice? What have you learned about yourself as a beginning teacher?

_____

_____

Review the *Key Questions* in the PLAN section of this chapter. Which questions are still confusing? List them below and set up a time to discuss them with your cooperating teacher or supervisor.

_____

_____

_____

✓ **Self-Reflection: Analyze Your Teaching Strategies to Enhance Student Learning** (Use the processes in Chapter 3 to guide your self-reflection.)

Which reflective tools did you use most often?_____

Why?_____

What did you learn about yourself as a teacher through this self-reflection process?

_____

_____

_____

✓ **Critique: Feedback from Your Supervisor and Cooperating Teacher to Guide Your Planning, Instructional Practice, and Professionalism**

Reread all of the critiques you received this semester (or year). Are there any themes? What do you notice about what has been observed about your practice and professionalism? How will you use this information?

_____

_____

_____

Chapter 10

Designing an Interview Portfolio

Where Do I Begin?

Focus on the students.

Student Teacher

An important tool for the job search will be the teacher portfolio you have been developing throughout the semester. This portfolio is sometimes known as a Professional Portfolio, an Employment Portfolio, a Presentation Portfolio, or a Certification Competency Portfolio. Whether or not you were required to complete it as part of your teacher preparation or state certification, you are encouraged to prepare one for your job interview process. If you are not applying for teaching positions right away, you should still complete your portfolio upon completion of student teaching while the experience is still fresh in your mind.

The portfolio should provide clear evidence of your teaching skills, abilities, and other attributes you bring to the profession. The collection of work is a visual display that illustrates your organizational skills and creativity. It should not be overwhelmingly large, nor should it hold all your teaching lessons. Rather it should be a "selective" representation of lessons and activities that highlight your strengths in a streamlined format. You may use any information from pre-practicum, full practicum, and teacher education courses and readings.

Even though the immediate purpose of the portfolio is to share your skills with a prospective employer, your portfolio is also a valuable professional development tool to maintain throughout your years of teaching. It is a place for you to collect and record your accomplishments as you move through your professional career. It can be shared with peers, parents, and principals. It can be displayed on "Open House" night to let new parents and students get to know you.

As a beginning teacher, you may be required to maintain a portfolio in addition to the formal evaluation by the principal. Evaluation is an important aspect of rehiring and obtaining professional status in your school district, and your portfolio can be useful in sharing what you are currently contributing to the school district.

You may choose to use an artist's case, a book bag, or a large easel pad to display your skills. Choose the presentation style that best reflects your area of teaching and your creative style. Early childhood teachers may prefer to create interactive portfolios that hold manipulatives they designed for their students. High school teachers may create a binder that reflects their subject area and age group. You may choose to include an "electronic computer portfolio" or video- or audiotapes as part of your presentation portfolio. Purchase a portfolio where you can add additional pages for easy addition of new information if you plan to add information in your beginning years.

The portfolio is the result of a process of gathering artifacts, thinking about why they represent your skills, and displaying them in a meaningful way. It represents learning and growth over time. Standardized tests for teacher competency measure one aspect of knowledge. The portfolio is an authentic assessment that allows the reviewer to gain an inside perspective of this teacher's thinking and her classroom. The process of creating the portfolio prepares you to share your teaching experience with a prospective employer in a thoughtful way. Some students have shared that in cases when they were not even asked to share their portfolio at the interview, they felt confident with the answers they gave to questions. Being prepared for the interview is key to responding confidently, and preparing the portfolio does prepare you.

Discussing Professional Standards

QUALITY CONVERSATIONS TO ENHANCE STUDENT LEARNING

National standards guide new teacher preparation in the United States. The INTASC created 10 principles for effective teaching. These principles are offered to you as a way to focus your attention on these key elements of practice. The "bottom line" is all about student learning. Are your students learning? How do you know?

Use these pages in each chapter to frame a quality conversation with your cooperating teacher and university supervisor. Don't be afraid to ask your own questions, too. Also use the REFLECT pages at the end of each chapter to deepen your thinking and to continue your quality conversations throughout the practium experience and into your first year of teaching.

INTASC Principles

Focus for Chapter 10

Review:
All Principles 1–10

ASK YOURSELF What do these principles mean to me right now? How will I know if I have achieved these principles?

DISCUSS WITH A PEER WHO IS ALSO PREPARING A JOB PORTFOLIO

How will we demonstrate our knowledge of the principles in our job interview portfolios? What evidence will we use to illustrate these skills?

How will we show that students have learned and will continue to learn as a result of our teaching?

PLAN

USE ADVICE FROM FORMER STUDENT TEACHERS

Talk to student teachers who have just completed the experience and review the tips below to guide you.

- Complete your portfolio as a visually pleasing document. Try to see other student teachers' portfolios.
- Use it in a job interview to answer questions!
- Keep the portfolio manageable! Less is more. It is not supposed to be a burden, but rather a celebration of your progress and work as a student teacher.

PROCESS YOUR EXPERIENCE

Respond to the Key Questions below by completing the process pages in each chapter. These ACTs will encourage you to deepen your thinking about teaching and learning. Write on the pages and save them to review at the end of the experience.

KEY QUESTIONS

1. How do I present my teaching philosophy?

2. How do I organize my portfolio?

3. What should I include in my portfolio?

4. What would a sample page look like?

5. How should I assess my portfolio?

PLAN

TAKE CARE OF YOURSELF AND AVOID STRESS

Plan to avoid the typical stresses of student teaching by following advice from cooperating teachers and university supervisors.

SEND A POSITIVE POSTCARD TO YOURSELF!

Invite students to write and send you a "Positive Postcard" about your teaching. Have them respond to prompts such as "I like it when you taught _____ because _____" or "I really enjoyed the day we _____ because _____" or any other compliment they have for you. This is not your student evaluation or assessment form to gain feedback about your teaching; this is simply a way to gather some positive information about you as a teacher.

PLAN YOUR WEEK

Priority List

Done	Tasks	Priority	Complete by When?

Place things to do on the day you would like to do them.

Monday Date:	Tuesday Date:	Wednesday Date:	Thursday Date:	Friday Date:

CONNECT

CONNECT is a resource page with ideas and suggestions to support you during student teaching. Select and complete any CONNECT items that will enhance your experience in the classroom.

CONNECT with people

- Teachers who have created portfolios
  Talk with teachers in your school or district who have completed portfolios for professional development or in-service. Ask them to share their portfolios with you.
- Student teachers who have created portfolios
  Seek out student teachers who completed portfolios last semester. What advice can they offer as you begin the process of putting yours together?

CONNECT with readings & resources

- Books and authors to explore on the Internet or at your local library
  How to Develop a Professional Portfolio by Campbell et al. (Allyn and Bacon)
  Creating Portfolios: For Success in School, Work, & Life by Kimeldorf (Free Spirit Press)
  Teacher Portfolios: Literary Artifacts and Themes by Rogers & Danielson (Heinemann)
  Portfolio Portraits by Graves and Sunstein (Heinemann)
  The Teacher Portfolio: A Strategy for Professional Development and Evaluation by Green and Symser (Technomic)

CONNECT technology to teaching

- Search
  Put the word out on the network that you are looking for portfolio tips and see what you find!
- Use an electronic portfolio program
  Scholastic offers a complete program and guide for creating an electronic version.

ACT
Process 10.1   Writing My Philosophy Statement

In the first chapter, you completed a form that started you thinking about your dispositions, assumptions, and beliefs about teaching. Reread your philosophy and compare it to how you see yourself now. Would you use the same words to describe yourself? Do you have the same beliefs? By now you should have many concrete ways in which you have demonstrated these beliefs in your classroom.

1. How have your descriptive words of yourself changed? Write down some new words you would use to describe yourself:

2. How have your assumptions changed? How have your beliefs changed? Or stayed the same?

3. List as many concrete examples as you can that relate to the description and beliefs you have written:

Use these examples as "artifacts" in your teacher portfolio.

After you have compared your original statements and added any new words, use these ideas to write a one-page philosophy statement that will appear as the front page of your portfolio. This will be the statement that is the foundation of your portfolio. All artifacts and examples will stem from this platform statement. Remember that your statement will be unique and will represent who you are as a teacher and how you see yourself.

ACT
Process 10.2A Organizing My Portfolio
Collect

Now it is time to review what you have collected and create a preliminary table of contents for your portfolio. If you are still in student teaching, you still have time to collect the items you may have forgotten.

INVENTORY OF POSSIBLE ARTIFACTS FOR PORTFOLIO

_____ Diagram of classroom (i.e., floor plan, photos, or both)

_____ Lesson plans highlighting any original work created by student teacher

_____ Unit plans integrating subject areas, including the arts, thematic, etc.

_____ Cooperative learning techniques

_____ Classroom management and discipline strategies

_____ Samples of student work; each subject area, advanced work, work adapted for diverse needs, homework, tests, artwork, performance assessment

_____ Audiotapes of students in groups; you introducing a lesson

_____ Videotapes (permission slip) of students during a lesson; documentary of classroom

_____ Materials from pre-practicum that may be highlighted

_____ Materials from methods course

_____ Photographs of classroom, bulletin boards, group lessons (permission slip of students)

_____ Documentation of any honors or awards

_____ Appreciation letters; notes from parents; notes from students

_____ Evaluations from others; cooperating teacher recommendation; supervisor evaluation

_____ Professional profile (third-person bio page) to go with résumé

_____ Books and articles read with how they helped you to be a better teacher

_____ Inspirational writings, poems, etc., that may serve as titles for pages or cover

_____ Other?

POSSIBLE TABLE OF CONTENTS

How will you sequence your items into a logical, meaningful format?

First Page-Teaching philosophy should be right up front!

ACT
Process 10.2B Organizing My Portfolio
Select

Selecting the work you will present in your portfolio can be difficult when you have so much to choose from, especially since you can use pre-practicum or teacher education items as well. Don't forget to delete names of students if you use samples of their work.

The portfolio is not a scrapbook or a complete documentation of your student teaching. Your student teaching binder should include all the requirements for student teaching, and the teacher portfolio should be a "showcase" of your work and reflections. Select a few examples or artifacts that illustrate your competencies. You don't need to display a lesson plan for every artifact in your portfolio—one or two are enough to demonstrate that you know how to plan and implement an effective lesson.

Ask yourself each time you want to put something into your portfolio, Is this already represented in what I have in here now?

GUIDELINES FOR SELECTING ARTIFACTS

1. Use your philosophy statement as a guide to selecting the examples you feel best represent who you are as a teacher.

   What **must** be in your portfolio?

2. Use professional standards.

   Demonstrating competency is a key purpose to organizing your portfolio. Select artifacts that will let the reader know you have met professional standards and are a competent and caring teacher. Sample professional standards for your state may include the following:

   Content Knowledge

   Use courses you have taken to illustrate how much you know. If you have to take a state exam, you may want to include your passing score.

   List other ideas that would show you have content knowledge here.

   Plans Curriculum and Instruction

   Use sample lesson plans, units, and curriculum you have designed to demonstrate what you have done during student teaching. Include assessments and ways you would use technology in your lessons.

   List examples of what you could include here.

Delivers Effective Instruction

Show samples of lessons you actually taught with examples of student work. Photographs of you in action with students will bring illustrate your skills. List specific ideas here.

Manages Classroom Climate and Operations

Show samples of your classroom routines as well as ways in which you work with students who may be disruptive. Demonstrate your competence in classroom management. List your ideas here.

Promotes Equity

Use samples of ways you thoughtfully organized your classroom for all learners. What else did you do to promote equity? List your examples here.

Meets Professional Responsibilities

Your understanding of the laws for special education students, as well as other laws that regulate teachers and practice, may be included in your portfolio. How you participated in your community of learners at the college or at the school as well as how you collaborated are important. Ways you consciously connected with parents should be listed, too. What will you include? List here.

3. Use examples of school of education themes.

Collaboration

Social justice in the classroom through service learning projects

Inquiry into practice

Reflection and how you included it in your student teaching

4. Use examples of how you used technology.

How skilled are you?

Your proficiency?

Web sites you have used

Electronic journaling

How can these four areas assist you in selecting your "best practice" as you begin to pull your portfolio together?

ACT
Process 10.2C Organizing My Portfolio
Reflect

Reflection is what defines your portfolio as different from a scrapbook. How have you been thinking about teaching during your student teaching?

REVIEW

1. Review your journals, looking for themes or ideas that you have been thinking about throughout the semester. Do any of these thoughts need to be articulated in your portfolio? Where would they fit? Do you need to summarize or can you excerpt a whole passage?

2. Review your bubble sheets. Are there any ideas you would like to share in your portfolio? Where would they fit?

3. Review any conversations you had with your supervisor or cooperating teacher. Think about what you have learned from the conversations. How might these words be displayed in your portfolio?

4. Review your philosophy statement. What might you want to use as a theme throughout your portfolio? Are there key words you want to emphasize?

WRITE

Each page in your portfolio should have a clearly defined title, a description of what is on the page, and a short reflective piece. Your reflections may be as short as one sentence or as long as a paragraph.

1. Shorten reflections and place near artifacts, lessons, and examples. Note: This is not your caption or description, but rather your thinking about teaching that tells the reviewer what you learned from teaching this, what you would do differently, what worked, and so on.

2. Include a one-page final reflection that serves as a "bookend" to your portfolio (the philosophy statement being the front bookend). Possible stems for writing such a piece could be
   - What I learned from student teaching
   - My goals and aspirations for teaching
   - My thoughts about teaching

As you begin to make decisions about what to include, your portfolio will "emerge" from the stacks of collected materials. Don't try to include everything! Remember, it is more powerful to include your words in the front and other people's words in the back. Reviewers expect the evaluations you select will be positive, so it is not necessary to put them up front. They are more interested in hearing what you have to say!

TABLE OF CONTENTS

_____ Philosophy Statement (one page)

_____ Professional Profile (third person; one paragraph)

Highlight your professionalism, additional activities, and strengths by including a professional profile in the portfolio. Like a biography, this narrative will provide your readers with highlights of your best features: languages you speak, places you have traveled, sports you play or coach, and skills you bring to teaching. Review your student teaching profile and résumé for ideas. Use an author's description on a book jacket to guide you.

_____ Instructional Practice

This will be the major portion of your portfolio. It should be organized by competencies and/or themes with reflections and descriptions.

See ACT Process 10.2 in this chapter for specific ideas:

  _____ Artifacts (photos, lesson plans, etc.)

  _____ Diagrams

  _____ Audio and video with written explanation of what is on the tape

  _____ Samples of student work

_____ Appreciation Notes, Public Appreciation (from parents, teachers, students)

If you saved notes people wrote to you that were positive, include them on a page titled Appreciation. If they relate to a lesson, you may include them on that page.

_____ Evaluation Reports (from supervisor and cooperating teacher)

_____ Guest Register (last page)

This page is for people to sign and date when they read it. Space for one brief comment should be included.

OPTIONAL

Create your own teaching trifold brochure highlighting your skills, goals, and attributes. Design it like a business brochure that is used to sell a service or product.

Create your own business card. Put several in the front pocket of your portfolio and include it in mailings or at the interview.

ACT
Process 10.4 Designing an INTASC Portfolio

The Interstate New Teacher Assessment & Support Consortium principles may guide the framework for your portfolio.

Review the 10 principles and decide which kinds of evidence would best document your practice. Use the principles as the scaffolding for your portfolio in a three-ring binder.

SAMPLE TABLE OF CONTENTS

Tab 1. Philosophy Statement and Photo with Cooperating Teacher

Tab 2. How I Have Changed from Beginning to End (assumptions, beliefs, etc.)

Tab 3–13 (Tab each Principle)

Principles #1–10 How do you demonstrate that you have met each of them?	Evidence and Reflections related to completion of this principle. 3–5 examples—lesson plans, process pages from this guide, photos, other descriptions, etc.

Tab 14. Summary of all inquiry journals

Check your portfolio for spelling and grammar. SHARE IT!

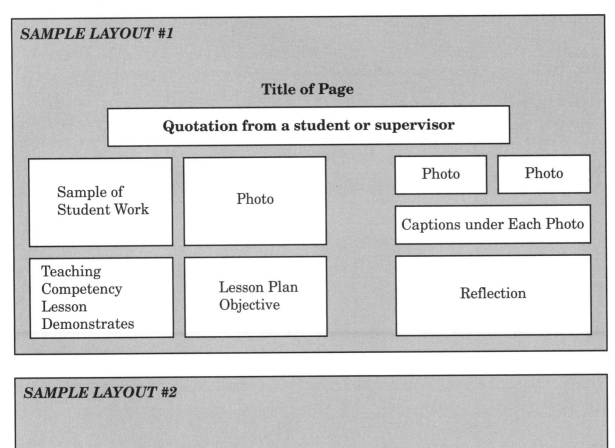

SAMPLE LAYOUT #1

Title of Page

Quotation from a student or supervisor

| Sample of Student Work | Photo | Photo | Photo |

Captions under Each Photo

| Teaching Competency Lesson Demonstrates | Lesson Plan Objective | Reflection |

SAMPLE LAYOUT #2

Theme of Teaching Competency Demonstrated

Photo and Caption

Examples of Student Work with Photos and Captions

Lesson Plan
Assessment of Lesson
What Did Students Learn?

Reflection of Lesson

ACT
Process 10.6   Creating a Mini-Portfolio Brochure

Creating an executive summary of your portfolio is a good idea. This reminds the committee of your qualifications and also allows you to continue to share your strengths in a visual format.

Two ideas to consider for executive summary options are:

1. **A tri-fold brochure highlighting your skills.**
   Consider including:
   - An eye-catching cover with your name, address, and E-mail
   - A brief summary of philosophy statement using key words or quotations
   - Photographs with students in your classroom
   - Testimony from others who have worked with you

   Review brochures from the business world to see layout options. Keep your brochure visually pleasing and colorful with lots of white space to catch the reader's attention. Note: This brochure can easily be reformatted as an introduction letter to be mailed to the parents of the students in your first class. Use one side of the tri-fold for mailing address. You may substitute a letter to the parents (or students) for the testimony sections.

2. **A streamlined version of your larger portfolio.**
   Consider including:
   - Cover letter written to this committee thanking them for the opportunity
   - Your philosophy statement or brochure (see above)
   - ONE lesson plan and a reflection of how you taught it
   - A photograph—(you in your classroom with students if possible)
   - A résumé
   - Optional: education business card

   Do not put TOO much in this summary portfolio!!!! It should be placed in a slim colorful cover with your CURRENT address and phone number so you can be reached easily. Optional: You may want to create your own educational business card! Don't forget to include your E-mail address. Add the card to your résumé and cover letters when applying for positions and include it in your portfolio and executive summary portfolio. Create a logo and have your portfolio match! Be creative!

Remember to bring enough copies for all members of the interview committee and leave the brochure or summary portfolio for them to keep!

REFLECT

Three ways you may use to reflect on your practice during student teaching are listed on this page. Select the methods of reflection that will stimulate your thinking. Write in an *Inquiry Journal* during student teaching. This writing will serve as a data source for solving problems over time. Uncover your own assumptions, biases, and dispositions as you write in your journal several times each week.

✓ **Inquiry: Teacher Research as a Tool for Solving Classroom Problems and Enhancing Student Learning**

What questions are arising as you design your interview portfolio? Who can help you answer these questions? What books or resources will assist you?

_____

_____

_____

Review the *Key Questions* in the PLAN section of this chapter. Which questions are still confusing? List them below and set up a time to discuss them with your cooperating teacher or supervisor.

_____

_____

_____

✓ **Self-Reflection: Analyze Your Teaching Strategies to Enhance Student Learning** (Use the processes in Chapter 3 to guide your self-reflection.)

How will you demonstrate your skills in self-reflection in your interview portfolio?

_____

_____

_____

✓ **Critique: Feedback from Your Supervisor and Cooperating Teacher to Guide Your Planning, Instructional Practice, and Professionalism**

How will you incorporate feedback given to you throughout the practicum into your teacher portfolio?

_____

_____

_____

Chapter 11

The Search for a Teaching Position

Where Do I Begin?

Organize! Organize! Organize!

Student Teacher

As you complete your student teaching experience, you will begin your search for your first teaching position. Integrate your job search activities throughout your student teaching by beginning your portfolio, writing your résumé, finding out what services the Career Center offers, and creating your own personal time line for being in a classroom of your own. When you complete student teaching, you can more actively submit letters of application, participate in interviews, and demonstrate your teaching with prospective employers.

The job search is an exciting and stressful time for a beginning professional. If you are open to relocating to parts of the country that have many teacher openings, your search may not be as difficult. If you are only interested in staying in your home town or state, you may have more of a challenge if the openings are not available. The international job market, private schools, and charter schools are all other possible places to seek teaching positions. The question you must ask yourself is "Where would I like to teach?" Set your goals for positions where you see yourself being personally and professionally satisfied.

There are resources to assist you in your search. You should seek out the Career Center or Job Placement Office located on your college campus. This office will provide information for you as you design a plan for seeking employment. These offices may offer meetings to help you write résumés and cover letters and complete applications. Another service may be to provide on-campus recruiting for local area towns that are seeking new teachers. Take advantage of all the services this office provides. Your own personal relationships and the connections you have made during student teaching are also valuable resources. Finding out where the openings are and when they will be posted is important as you set your personal time line for employment.

If you graduate from your teacher preparation program in May, you most likely will be looking for a job for September. School districts typically hire in the summer when the school budgets have been finalized and when teachers have made final decisions about retirements. Some new teachers are hired as late as the first day of school. However, with the trend toward needing teachers in some specific subject areas, you may notice that jobs are being posted earlier in the year.

If you graduate in December, you may still be seeking a full-time job for the next year, but you have a chance to review the options and perhaps substitute teach in districts where you feel employment may be forthcoming. Your time line has to match your life's objectives. When do you want to be in a classroom? When will districts be hiring? How long do you wait? Are you willing to substitute teach first?

Organizing and implementing an effective job search will offer you more choices for teaching positions. Selecting where you will start your professional career is an important life decision. Use these pages to guide you.

Discussing Professional Standards

QUALITY CONVERSATIONS TO ENHANCE
STUDENT LEARNING

National standards guide new teacher preparation in the United States. The INTASC created 10 principles for effective teaching. These principles are offered to you as a way to focus your attention on these key elements of practice. The "bottom line" is all about student learning. Are your students learning? How do you know?

Use these pages in each chapter to frame a quality conversation with your cooperating teacher and university supervisor. Don't be afraid to ask your own questions, too. Also use the REFLECT pages at the end of each chapter to deepen your thinking and to continue your quality conversations throughout the practium experience and into your first year of teaching.

INTASC Principles

Focus for Chapter 11

Review:
All Principles 1–10

ASK YOURSELF   What do these principles mean to me right now? How will I know if I have achieved these principles?

DISCUSS WITH OTHER STUDENT TEACHERS

How will prospective employers know if you have achieved these principles? What evidence will you have to demonstrate these skills to them?

How will you explain that your students have learned as a result of your teaching?

PLAN

USE ADVICE FROM FORMER STUDENT TEACHERS

Talk to student teachers who have just completed the experience and review the tips below to guide you.

- Network with people at your student teaching site and at your university.
- Highlight your skills and ability to solve problems as a beginning teacher using an inquiry approach.
- Seek teaching positions that match your philosophy and preparation.

PROCESS YOUR EXPERIENCE

Respond to the Key Questions below by completing the process pages in each chapter. These ACTs will encourage you to deepen your thinking about teaching and learning. Write on the pages and save them to review at the end of the experience.

KEY QUESTIONS

1. How do I find a job opening?

2. How do I apply for a potential position?

3. How do I prepare for the interview?

4. What is a demonstration lesson?

5. How do I choose if I have more than one option?

6. What does signing a contract mean?

7. What do I do first after accepting a position?

PLAN

TAKE CARE OF YOURSELF AND AVOID STRESS

Plan to avoid the typical stresses of student teaching by following advice from cooperating teachers and university supervisors.

TREAT YOURSELF!

You have been working really hard and now it is time to enjoy something for fun!

- Go to a sports event.
- Attend a play or concert
- Get a new hair cut.
- Go away for the weekend.

What would be a real treat for you? Do that!

PLAN YOUR WEEK

Priority List

Done	Tasks	Priority	Complete by When?

Place things to do on the day you would like to do them.

Monday Date:	Tuesday Date:	Wednesday Date:	Thursday Date:	Friday Date:

CONNECT

CONNECT is a resource page with ideas and suggestions to support you during student teaching. Select and complete any CONNECT items that will enhance your experience in the classroom.

CONNECT with people

- Administrators in the school and district
  Talk with the principal at your student teaching site to gain advice about the job search in the district and the surrounding towns. Ask for her advice in the job search.
- Personal networks
  Review all the people you know who may have a "connection" to a school. Call to find out where the jobs are and ask whether they will give you a positive word.

CONNECT with readings & resources

- Check with the Career Planning Office to find most current books
- Read the latest issue of *ASCUS ANNUAL: A Job Search Handbook for Educators,* published by the Association for School, College, and University Staffing, 301 South Swift Road, Addison, IL 60101.

CONNECT technology to teaching

- Career centers
  Most are posting jobs on their websites—check here first
- Department of Education Job Employment Matching website
  Find the local address for your state
- Local school district postings on the Web
  Local districts are beginning websites—see whether the towns you are looking for are on the Internet.
- Other possible positions
  Use the leads in this chapter to search the Web for possible positions

ACT
Process 11.1   Teaching Positions—Where to Find Them

You need to put a conscious systematic effort into discovering where teaching jobs are being posted. You may want to teach in your own hometown, but there may not be any openings right now. You could opt to substitute teach to get your foot in the door and wait for a teaching position, or you could branch out and teach in a neighboring district and transfer into your own town when openings become available. Remember, openings for teaching positions are created by (1) teachers retiring from existing positions and (2) growing districts adding new schools and teachers. Read the newspaper and real estate guides to see where towns are growing or where there are numbers of retiring teachers.

PLACES THAT CAN POINT YOU TO JOB OPENINGS

_____ The Career Center or University Job Placement Office upcoming job fairs, résumé matches, job listings on the website

_____ Newspaper ads
Sunday newspapers usually list openings for positions in the geographic area

_____ State Department of Education and Bureau of Teacher Certification list of openings on the website for schools or at Department of Education list of towns where new schools are being built

_____ State Employment Office and federal government teaching in correctional institutions, Bureau of Indian Affairs, and other government agencies related to education

_____ State Teachers' Union and Teachers' Retirement Board may have a job-matching system that shows where openings are due to retirement

_____ U.S. Department of Defense (DOD) schools
Office of Overseas Dependent Schools, 2461 Eisenhower Ave., Alexandria, VA 22331

_____ Office of Overseas Schools
Room 234, SA-6 Department of State, Washington, DC 20520

_____ Real estate groups
Realtors will have information about schools and where new ones are being built

_____ Personal networks
Ask your parents, your friends who are teachers, the school you attended, where you student taught, etc.

Applying for a Position

There are teaching positions all over the United States and the world. What are you looking for?

☐ Public school?
☐ Independent school?
☐ Religiously affiliated school?
☐ International school?

You need to find out how the positions are being posted. Are they listed by the central office, by the superintendent of schools, or by the building principals who do the hiring? Do they require a letter or an application? Do private schools have a different procedure for application? Your university career center may be able to guide you in learning about the districts and schools in which you are most interested.

Applications for positions may be completed by...

1. Responding to an official opening posted in the newspaper for a specific position needed:
   Specific details and job requirements will be listed. See how closely you match the description and respond if you fit the bill or if you come close.

2. Attending on-campus recruiting sessions with districts that are in need of teachers:
   Typically, school personnel arrive on campus and spend a day doing short interviews. This screening process allows districts to see a large number of student teachers and allows student teachers to interview with a variety of districts in a short time. Usually résumés are sent to the districts through the career center and the districts select students to be interviewed. After initial interview at the college, school personnel call back students they would like to have come to the school site for a second interview.

3. Exploring in a district/region/state where you would like to teach:
   This could be your own hometown or a geographic area in the state that you have decided on. This is where student teachers who don't do their homework tend to get frustrated if they blindly mail hundreds of résumés out and don't hear anything. Focus on towns/areas that have retiring teachers or that are building new schools.

Which type of process would you like to pursue?

_____

_____

ACT
Process 11.2B The Application Process
The Cover Letter

Your cover letter is perhaps the most important piece of your application packet, because it is the first impression you give to the hiring committee. Every résumé you send should be accompanied by a cover letter. The purpose of the letter is to introduce yourself, arouse the reader's interest, and persuade the person reading the letter to interview you. If you are responding to an official job posting or ad, state that clearly. If you are writing a letter of inquiry about possible jobs, state that. Sample cover letters should be available in your college career planning and placement office.

TIPS FOR SUCCESSFUL COVER LETTERS

- Personalize the letter.

    Use the name of the district and person who is doing the hiring whenever possible. If you use parts of the letter as a template, be sure to review it carefully and change the names from previous letters!

- Proofread for perfect grammar and spelling.

    Before mailing have someone carefully edit and check for errors.

- Limit the cover letter to one page.

    Emphasize your teaching experiences, special interests, and reasons you are the best candidate for the district.

- Include your *permanent* address, phone, and E-mail.

    You may be in transition, so make sure the address you list is one that you would consider permanent. Change your voice mail or answering machine if it is not appropriate.

- Refer to your teacher portfolio.

    At the end of the letter state that you have a teacher portfolio and would be happy to share it at an interview. This is a "hook" to create interest to gain an interview.

Sample Outline for a Cover Letter

Paragraph 1	• Why you are writing this letter (i.e., responding to a posting or exploration of possible position that may open in the near future). If it is a response to a posting, *clearly identify the position.*
	• What you already know about the district via the Internet or other connection and why it is a match for you.
Paragraph 2	Your interest in becoming a teacher (i.e., beliefs about teaching).
Paragraph 3	Teacher preparation program, qualifications, and student teaching experience.
Paragraph 4	Request interview, refer to enclosed résumé, refer to portfolio available at interview, and include a thank you.

ACT
Process 11.2C The Application Process
The Résumé

Your résumé should be no more than two pages on either white or off-white paper. Design a résumé format that is uncluttered and easy to read. Remember, you may be one of hundreds applying for a position and you want to have your material read. Clear and concise is always better than a wordy narrative. Look for the "white space" to see how your layout appeals to the eye. Review sample copies of résumés available in your career center or field office. Ask students who have recently completed the job search to share their résumé formats with you.

Possible Headings for an Education Résumé

Name: _____ **Current Address:** _____

Permanent Address: _____ **E-mail:** _____

Check the headings that you would consider for your résumé.

☐ Professional objective
☐ Education (undergraduate, graduate)
☐ Teacher preparation courses (highlight special ones that may make you different)
☐ Teaching experience (pre-practicum, full practicum, other)
☐ Related experience
☐ College activities
☐ Leadership skills
☐ Volunteer experience
☐ Language proficiency
☐ Honors and awards or achievements
☐ Computer skills
☐ Portfolio
☐ References available upon request

- Don't include personal data, such as age, height, family status, or a photograph on your résumé.
- Do list experiences in reverse chronological order.

ACT
Process 11.2D The Application Process
The School's Application

Some school districts require candidates to complete the district's own application in addition to sending in the résumé and cover letter. If the position is posted in the newspaper, it may state to call for an application. If it does not state that there is a town application, you can assume a cover letter and résumé is sufficient.

Keep a record of the districts to which you have applied and what specific materials are required. Write the date in the box when you send the material.

School/ District	Contact Person	Application	Cover Letter	Résumé	Portfolio	Demonstration Lesson	Other Information

Note: You may want to mail your information certified mail with a return receipt. This relieves some of your anxiety and lets you know when and who received the mailing.

After you have mailed your materials to a school district or principal, you will be anxious to hear from them. If you mailed your materials using a return receipt, you will know exactly when it was received. However, you won't know when the committee will meet and review the qualified candidates and set up interviews.

Wait a few weeks and if you have not heard what the procedure for selecting will be, you may want to place a courtesy phone call to the district secretary. There is no need to talk directly with the principal or superintendent, because they may not be part of the process at this time. The secretary or the human resources department in larger cities usually take care of the details for setting up interviews and are aware of the time lines in a school for hiring. If the voice-mail system is automated and you find you cannot connect with a live person, you may want to ask for the person who signed your return-receipt slip.

When making this call, be clear, cheerful, and short. Ask if the packet has been received, if they need any other information is needed, and when you might expect a call or letter regarding an interview. If the person does not know, thank him for his time and ask whether there is someone you should be talking with. The goal is just to give you a time frame and a procedure that you can expect. If the school is not interviewing for two more months, you can relax!

Typically, the larger the district, the longer the process. If you are working through the process in a city with a human resources division that is taking applications for hundreds of schools, you can expect delays. On the other hand, a small school where the principal does the hiring directly could move more quickly.

District/ School	Application Process	Date Application Sent	Date Received by District	Date of Follow-Up Phone Call	Notes

ACT
Process 11.3   The Interview

Congratulations! You have made it through the first hoop, and you have been invited to be interviewed at the school. Either you mailed your materials directly to the school or you participated in an on-campus recruiting session, and the district wants to know more about you.

PREPARING FOR THE INTERVIEW

- Research the school on its website.
- Talk with students from your college who are teaching to gain insights.
- Attend an interview workshop if one is available on campus.
- Find out who will be at the interview (e.g., one person, a committee, and/or parents).
- Review and role-play potential interview questions (audiotape or videotape).
- Review your philosophy statement, your portfolio contents, and your résumé.
- Plan your interview attire (suit or dress with jacket).
- Think about questions you would ask them.
- Prepare packets for people who will be at the interview (see ACT Process 10.6).

SAMPLE QUESTIONS YOU MAY BE ASKED

1. What do you consider your strengths as a teacher?
2. How would you plan a lesson for _____ subject?
3. How do you engage students in learning?
4. How do you assess student learning?
5. What procedures do you use for classroom management and discipline?
6. Describe two mistakes in teaching you have made and how you solved them.
7. What three words describe you as a teacher?
8. What do you believe about teaching and learning?
9. Describe your content area strengths.
10. Why should we hire you?
11. What are the reasons for your college success?
12. Why do you want to work at this school/in this district?

Before the Interview

Interviewers are looking for teachers who . . .

- Will fit into an existing school system culture.
- Will be enthusiastic about teaching.
- Will go the extra mile for the students.
- Can relate to parents and other teachers.
- Will be contributing members of the school.

The Day of the Interview

- Be on time! Drive to the school the day before so you know exactly where it is.
- Dress professionally—a suit is best.
- Shake hands as you meet administrators and teachers.
- Make eye contact throughout the interview.
- Be yourself—smile, be positive, be passionate about teaching.
- *Listen* carefully to the questions before responding.
- Ask for clarification if you don't understand a question.
- Bring your portfolio—integrate it when appropriate.
- Optional: Bring executive summary of portfolio to leave.

Other things you could expect at an interview:

- A writing sample may be requested on the spot. Samples are often related to a scenario of how to handle a teaching situation.
- Questions from you are often expected. One or two are enough!

Possible questions to ask at the interview:

1. What are you most proud of in your school/district?
2. What types of assessments are required for students?
3. How is teacher professional development encouraged?
4. How are new teachers oriented and mentored?
5. Which curriculum areas/classes/grades would I be hired for?
6. When will the decision be made?

Leave the interview site confidently as soon as you have finished. Do not stay and talk with candidates who are waiting to be interviewed.

Follow-Up to the Interview

- Evaluate the interview. Your notes and reflections of what happened at the interview are important. As soon as you leave, write as many questions as you can remember in an interview notebook. Each interview you participate in helps you to gain confidence and skills in sharing yourself.

- Write a short thank-you note. If you want to write to all members of the committee, call the school secretary the next day to obtain correct names with titles and spellings.

Letters or phone calls from the district/school indicate your next steps. A phone call is usually positive, and you may be asked for a second interview or a demonstration lesson. Rejection usually comes in the form of a letter. If you are rejected, think about what you learned from the experience and *move on to the next interview.* You may want to talk with the principal or committee chair to ask how you could improve your presentation.

After each interview, note the questions asked in a notebook. What do you recall?

ACT
Process 11.4 Preparing and Teaching
a Demonstration Lesson

As part of the application process, student teachers may be asked to demonstrate their teaching skills in front of an interview committee.

CHECKLIST FOR A SUCCESSFUL DEMONSTRATION LESSON

Preparing for a Demonstration Lesson

- Ask the committe what it would like you to teach. If there is a choice, choose a lesson that you have already successfully implemented.
- Prepare a long lesson plan to show the committee your planning skills. Pace the lesson for the time frame offered; don't pack in too much. Make sure you have 10 minutes for the closing.
- Integrate strategies for diverse learners.
- Ask if you can have the names of the students or name cards before you teach.
- Ask if there are any particular student needs or issues that you should prepare for.

What to Do at the School Site

- Show off what you can do!
    Use visuals
    Use technology
    Engage students
- Arrive early at the site and view the room organization.
- Meet the teacher and committee and share your plan. Have extra copies for all viewers.
- Teach the lesson!
- Clean up your materials.
- Have a follow-up conversation with the committee. Ask if the committee has any questions.

Note: Sometimes the school wants to videotape these demonstration lessons for members of the committee who can't be there. Don't be nervous—share your skills!

ACT
Process 11.5   Selecting a District That's Right for Me

To be successful as a teacher and to remain in the profession, you need to have your personal and professional needs met. The position you select may become your teaching position for many years to come. It is important to select a system that is a good match for you and not to jump into a job just because it was offered to you.

Even if you don't have a choice of positions, you should ask yourself the following about the position you have been offered so there will be no surprises in your first year.

WORKING CONDITIONS

Is there positive support for teachers in the school?

How do teachers relate to parents?

Would you have a mentor teacher assisting you?

BENEFITS

Salary	Sick days
Job security	Medical insurance
Promotion opportunities	Dental insurance
Schedule	Professional development
Vacations	

MATCH FOR YOUR PERSONAL GOALS

Does the school/district match your goal for type of school: public, private, international?

Does the district/school support the success of beginning teachers?

Does the district/school match your teaching philosophy?

All three areas are important, and there is no one way to analyze your answers. If the district is a 100 percent match for you, you will be very lucky, but often there will be areas that are not up to your needs. For example, one district may pay less than another but it provides a more positive working condition. You are the only person who can decide which will meet your needs in the long run and support you staying in the profession.

Analyzing the answers to these questions will be important. A key question is "Does the district provide a mentor teacher to support you during the first year?"

If you have more than one choice, make a list of each school's advantages and disadvantages. Then think about your "intrinsic" rewards that you are looking for. Does this match your philosophy? Good Luck.

ACT
Process 11.6   Professional Ethics and Signing a Contract

Public school employees in most states have contract agreements with their local school boards that list their salaries and benefits. Ask for a copy of the contract when you are asked to sign your agreement. If you seek employment in private or international schools, there may be other forms of agreement.

Review contracts before signing them. If you are not sure about some language, ask if you can take it home to review it. *DO NOT SIGN if you are not sure* or if you have other offers pending. Be open and tell the district or school you are waiting to hear from another district, and ask if you may have a few more days.

Ethics are involved in making and keeping an agreement. When you sign a contract, you are stating to the school district that you have made a commitment to the students in the classroom that you will be assigned. Breaking a contract is a serious matter. Breaking a contract because another job comes along that pays a higher salary or offers other benefits is an ethical issue. Think of the agreement in reverse: How would you feel if the district came back to you several months later and said they had found a stronger candidate and were letting you go?

Be sure your commitment is with this district before your pen touches the paper.

How will you decide whether you will sign a contract?

_____

_____

_____

_____

_____

_____

_____

_____

_____

_____

_____

ACT
Process 11.7 Accepting My First Teaching Position

Congratulations!

You have accepted your first teaching position, and now it is time to set up your very own classroom.

A CHECKLIST

☐ **Visit the school.**
- Introduce yourself to all the important people (see your list from this text).
- Ask for school handbooks, curriculum guides, and policies (same as student teaching).
- Ask how you receive materials and supplies.

☐ **Visit your classroom.**
- Inventory what you have (e.g., books, materials, supplies).
- Draw a floor plan.
- List of what you will need.

☐ **Meet with the principal/department chair.**
- Make an appointment to talk.
- Ask when school begins.
- Ask when you can be in the building.

☐ **Meet the teacher union representatives.**
- Ask about membership.
- Ask if there is a new-teacher orientation.
- Obtain a contract.
- Ask for a list of other benefits.

☐ **Meet your mentor teacher.**
- Find out whether she is assigned or a volunteer.
- Exchange phone numbers.
- Ask details of support program.

☐ **Other?**

REFLECT

Three ways you may use to reflect on your practice during student teaching are listed on this page. Select the methods of reflection that will stimulate your thinking. Write in an *Inquiry Journal* during student teaching. This writing will serve as a data source for solving problems over time. Uncover your own assumptions, biases, and dispositions as you write in your journal several times each week.

✓ **Inquiry: Teacher Research as a Tool for Solving Classroom Problems and Enhancing Student Learning**

What questions are arising as you prepare for the job search? How will you CONNECT to the resources, people, and use technology to assist you?

_____

_____

_____

Review the *Key Questions* in the PLAN section of this chapter. Which questions are still confusing? List them below and set up a time to discuss them with colleagues or university faculty.

_____

_____

_____

_____

✓ **Self-Reflection: Analyze Your Teaching Strategies to Enhance Student Learning** (Use the processes in Chapter 3 to guide your self-reflection.)

How will you describe your ability to use self-reflection as an asset to being hired by any school district?

_____

_____

_____

✓ **Critique: Feedback from Your Supervisor and Cooperating Teacher to Guide Your Planning, Instructional Practice, and Professionalism**

Teacher evaluation is a component of the job. As you search for a teaching position how will you explain in an interview to a prospective employer how you will use her critique to impact your practice?

_____

_____

_____

_____

Chapter 12

Lifelong Learning for a Career in Teaching

How Do I Stay Current and Excited about Teaching?

Jump into your long awaited first year with both feet and hands, an open mind, a loving heart, and your entire soul.

Student Teacher

As you begin your professional career, you must remember to stay updated about new teaching methods, new information in your subject, and new ways to work with your students. Technology has brought educators closer to new information by way of the Internet. But the Internet alone will not provide you with enthusiasm and connections to people who make a difference. That is why you should continue to read, take courses, and participate in summer institutes. Joining committees at your school, taking on a leadership role in the teachers' union, joining a professional organization, or collaborating with other beginning teachers are ways in which you can be a part of the profession.

Teaching is difficult and rewarding work. As a beginning teacher, you will face the realities of children and families every day. The first year can be very isolating, because you are with the students alone without a cooperating teacher to guide you. Coping with the stresses of your daily schedule, taking care of yourself, and participating in your continued growth and development are important to your well-being and retention in the profession.

Many teachers leave the profession within the first three years because they feel unsupported and overwhelmed. Think about what you require for support and ask for assistance. Experienced teachers are there to help. You also need to think about ways in which you can be proactive to create a support network of beginning teachers in your school or district. It can be fun to meet weekly and share ideas and support each other through the growing pains.

You will move through many stages as a teacher. The beginning years serve as your induction into the profession and may be the most difficult for you. As you struggle with your classroom management, new curriculum, and new work environment, remember the difference you are making in your students' lives. Setting high standards for learning and maintaining your vision are valuable contributions to the profession. You bring enthusiasm, dreams, and new ideas to the schools. Don't give up if you don't reach all your goals the first year! Work with the experienced teachers, listen, learn, and reflect on the ideas you bring.

This chapter will provide you with an overview of the resources available to teachers. Participating fully in every aspect of your professional career means continuing to learn, grow, and reflect on your own practice. Welcome to the profession. You *do* make a difference.

Discussing Professional Standards

*QUALITY CONVERSATIONS TO ENHANCE
STUDENT LEARNING*

National standards guide new teacher preparation in the United States. The INTASC created 10 principles for effective teaching. These principles are offered to you as a way to focus your attention on these key elements of practice. The "bottom line" is all about student learning. Are your students learning? How do you know?

Use these pages in each chapter to frame a quality conversation with your cooperating teacher and university supervisor. Don't be afraid to ask your own questions, too. Also use the REFLECT pages at the end of each chapter to deepen your thinking and to continue your quality conversations throughout the practium experience and into your first year of teaching.

INTASC Principles

Focus for Chapter 12

Principle #9 The teacher is a reflective practitioner who continually evaluates the effects of his or her choices and actions of others (students, parents, and other professionals in the learning community) and who actively seeks out opportunities to grow professionally.

Principle #10 *The teacher fosters relationships with school colleagues, parents, and agencies in the larger community to support students' learning and well-being.*

ASK YOURSELF What do these principles mean to me right now? How will I know if I have achieved these principles?

*DISCUSS WITH YOUR MENTOR TEACHER IN
YOUR FIRST YEAR OF TEACHING*

How will your principal or department chair teacher know if you have achieved these principles? What evidence will you have to demonstrate these skills to them?

How will you know if your students have learned as a result of your teaching?

PLAN

USE ADVICE FROM FORMER STUDENT TEACHERS

Talk to student teachers who have just completed the experience and review the tips below to guide you.

- Find a mentor in your school and set up times to talk about teaching!
- Use the Internet to stay "connected" to the most current information.
- Read! Read! Read!
- Enjoy the profession you have chosen!

PROCESS YOUR EXPERIENCE

Respond to the Key Questions below by completing the process pages in each chapter. These ACTs will encourage you to deepen your thinking about teaching and learning. Write on the pages and save them to review at the end of the experience.

KEY QUESTIONS

1. What resources are available to assist me in my continued professional growth?

2. What can I expect from my new colleagues and what will they expect of me?

3. How can a school mentor or team of mentors assist me?

4. How can I stay connected to my teacher education program?

5. What is a professional development plan?

6. What is recertification and how do I recertify?

7. What are my goals and aspirations for teaching?

PLAN

TAKE CARE OF YOURSELF AND AVOID STRESS

Plan to avoid the typical stresses of student teaching by following advice from cooperating teachers and university supervisors.

CELEBRATE YOUR PROGRESS!

As you end the semester and look ahead to your first position as a teacher, remind yourself of the good things. It is easier to focus on the negative sometimes because it surfaces in many ways. Reread all the "Care for Yourself" sections of this text to focus on the ways in which you have maintained a positive and healthy outlook for beginning your first year of teaching.

What do you feel good about?

PLAN YOUR WEEK

Priority List

Done	Tasks	Priority	Complete by When?

Place things to do on the day you would like to do them.

Monday Date:	Tuesday Date:	Wednesday Date:	Thursday Date:	Friday Date:

CONNECT

CONNECT is a resource page with ideas and suggestions to support you during student teaching. Select and complete any CONNECT items that will enhance your experience in the classroom.

CONNECT with people

- Community members
  Talk with people in the town to learn about the school through their eyes.

- Teacher education faculty and field experiences office
  Let us know where you are! We want to support you and connect with you! You are alumni now!

- Principals and department chairs
  Seek out ways in which you can participate in the school (e.g., club advisor, coaching, honors clubs, yearbook, drama).

CONNECT with readings & resources

- Professional development centers in your state
  Check out developmental centers, such as the Massachusetts Field Center for Teaching and Learning located at UMASS Boston. Write to UMASS to receive a free newsletter that includes many grants, events, workshops, and more!

- Books and authors to explore on the Internet or at your local library
  Surviving Your First Year of Teaching: Guidelines for Success by Kellough (Merrill)
  A Handbook for Beginning Teachers, 2nd ed. by MacDonald and Healy (Longman)
  The First Year of Teaching and Beyond by Kronowitz (Longman)
  The First Days of School by Wong (Wong Publications)
  The Unauthorized Teacher's Survival Guide by Warner and Bryan (Park Avenue)

CONNECT technology to teaching

- Your own webpage
  Create your own webpage for parents and students to read!

- Help for new, student, and mentoring teachers = http://www.inspiringteachers.com

- Tips and strategies from first-year teachers =
  http://www.ed.gov/pubs/FirstYear/ch3.html

- More websites to review
  Busy Teacher's Website = http://www.ceismc.gatech.edu/busyt/homepg.htm
  Teachers Helping Teachers = http://www.pacificnet.net/~mandel

ACT
Process 12.1 Resources for Professional Growth and Development

PROFESSIONAL ORGANIZATIONS AND PUBLICATIONS

There are many organizations for teachers today, ranging from early childhood to secondary subjects. These organizations have local, state, and national conferences and workshops. Most have a professional journal that keeps you updated on current research and practice. Check with your school librarian to find out which organizations the school may already be a member of and which journals are in the library for your use.

LIST OF SOME PROFESSIONAL ORGANIZATIONS

Association of Supervision and Curriculum Development

Association for Early Childhood Education

International Reading Association

National Council for Social Studies

National Council of Teachers of English

National Council of Teachers of Mathematics

National Science Teachers Association

In addition, a weekly education newspaper called *Education Week* highlights national and state news related to education issues.

Also, a variety of teacher magazines provide practical tips, teacher talk columns, units, lesson plans, and hands-on ideas. Check with your local school library for details.

Which journals, organizations, or magazines appeal to you? _____

_____

PROFESSIONAL TEACHERS' UNIONS

The two large general professional organizations are the National Education Association (NEA) and the American Federation of Teachers (AFT). The NEA was formed to promote professional development and improve teaching practices through collective bargaining. AFT functions primarily as a labor union to raise salaries and improve working conditions. Your school district may be associated with either the NEA or the AFT through its state affiliate. Talk with the union members in your school to find out more about the professional opportunities available through the teachers' associations.

What are the benefits for teacher members?_____

_____

ACT
Process 12.2 Expectations—What Can I Learn from Them?

Recently I conducted an informal survey of 35 beginning teachers from eight school districts as part of a mentoring support group established for the school year. When asked the following questions, the beginning teachers responded with these answers.

As you read the questions, think about how you would respond to each one and how these expectations you bring to your new position affect your views of teaching.

QUESTIONS TO BEGINNING TEACHERS

1A. What behaviors do you expect from *other teachers* at your new school?

Support, willingness to share, ideas, resources, help with long-term planning, acceptance, approachability, constructive criticism, include me socially, allow me freedom to teach my own way and learn through my mistakes

1B. What behaviors do you think other teachers *expect from you* as a beginning teacher?

To share new knowledge and methods, to put best foot forward, to have questions and to ask them, to fit in, to be receptive, to be professional, to respect their time constraints

2A. What behaviors do you expect from *other beginning teachers* at your new school?

Comradery and support, sharing materials, sharing ideas, a shoulder to lean or cry on, feedback, an opportunity to coplan and share lesson plans

2B. What behaviors do you think other beginning teachers *expect from you* as a beginning teacher?

Comradery and support, sharing materials, sharing ideas, a shoulder to lean or cry on, feedback, a sense of humor!

3A. What behaviors do you expect from your *school administrators?*

Support, information, reasonable class size, invitations to workshops, professional respect, support with discipline, professional guidance, empowerment, flexible evaluations, constructive criticism, positive reinforcement

3B. What behaviors do you think your school administrators *expect from you?*

Professionalism, control of class, good lesson plans with objectives, good judgment with discipline, communication with parents, current on education reform and professional development, positive attitude with staff, children, and parents

What are your personal expectations?

Do your expectations and thoughts match any of those from other beginning teachers?

Process 12.3 The Role of Mentor Teachers in My Development

You may be assigned a mentor at your school. This person will serve as a guide, a coach, and a person who will orient you to the culture of the school. If your assigned mentor does not deal with curriculum issues, you may also seek out an academic mentor who is familiar with your content area and can assist you with instruction.

Beginning teachers can also assist you because they are closest to your situation. It is preferable to have a team of people who assist you in different ways. Seek out the assistance you need and create your own support team.

Formal Mentor Assigned by School District

Name: _____   Phone Number: _____

Role of the Mentor: _____

Need Mentor Is Meeting: _____

Your Role: _____

Informal Mentor(s) You Select

Name: _____ Phone Number: _____

Name: _____ Phone Number: _____

Role of the Mentor(s): _____

Need Mentor(s) Is (Are) Meeting: _____

Your Role: _____

How do you see a mentor supporting you in your classroom?

Do you have a mentor from your college/university? How will this person support you?

Process 12.4 Staying Connected to My Teacher Preparation Program

Your teacher preparation program at the college or university you attended knows you and is a link to your professional life. Ask the professors and field office personnel how students can stay connected through an alumni link. Ask if there are chat rooms, beginning teacher meetings, or other supports in place for you as a beginning teacher. Let everyone know where you are working! Send a postcard to the school informing them of your teaching position.

If you stay near the college, you can stay connected to . . .

1. **People you know in teacher education**
   - Course work
     Stay connected to faculty to receive any new information.
   - Fieldwork
     The university supervisor knows you and has seen you teach—stay in touch.
     Your cooperating teacher can offer moral support during your first year—call her.

2. **Courses offered at the college**
   - Register for summer institutes
   - Other courses
   - Master's degree programs

3. **Events**
   - Attend events hosted at the college for beginning teachers.
   - Use E-mail to stay connected if you live far away.

Can you think of other ways you can stay connected to your teacher education program?

How can these connections support you?

Process 12.5   Creating a Professional Development Plan

Districts often require a professional development plan to document your goals and objectives for professional growth. Self-directed study may be a part of your professional plan. It allows you to choose the topics in which you are most interested. For example, an elementary teacher has to teach all subject areas, but you may particularly love teaching math and science. Your professional goal for the first year could be to focus on these areas because you find them fun! A secondary major who is teaching history may really love the Civil War, and that could be the focus of her professional development.

Self-directed study could result in a product, such as a curriculum unit, developed from a trip you took, other published materials, software packages, masters' theses, or work in some kind of business or community improvement service learning activity. You might develop a plan for having your students work with the elderly and design a unit around this.

Sometimes teachers are part of study groups or teacher research groups as part of their personal self-directed study. Other teachers conduct workshops for teachers or join reading groups in which everyone reads books and journals related to classroom practice.

Professional Development Plan

Date: _____

Goals for School Year: _____

_____

Self-Directed Activities: _____

_____

Required Activities: _____

_____

Ways Activities Affected Classroom Teaching: _____

_____

Process 12.6   Recertification—How Do I Apply?

Many states require teachers to recertify every five years or less. This means that teachers may have to take courses or complete independent projects to renew their teaching licenses. Your professional development plan may even be required for recertification in your state. Check with your Department of Education to receive a list of recertification requirements.

State recertification requirements:

_____

_____

How do you have to document your activities for recertification?

_____

_____

When will you need to submit paperwork for recertification? _____

Professional Plan Activity Schedule

Activity	Description	Started Date	Completed Date

Process 12.7 My Professional Goals and Aspirations

As you complete your student teaching and accept your first teaching position, take the time to think about your future. Really *listen* to your inner voice and record your dreams and visions for teaching for the first two years.

Goals for first year:

_____

_____

_____

Goals for second year:

_____

_____

_____

Where do I see myself in five years?

Ten years?

Complete this sheet and put it in a safe place for a year. Take it out at the end of your first year and see how well your goals match the reality.

Draw a picture as you imagine yourself in your first teaching position classroom.

Good luck!

REFLECT

Three ways you may use to reflect on your practice during student teaching are listed on this page. Select the methods of reflection that will stimulate your thinking. Write in an *Inquiry Journal* during student teaching. This writing will serve as a data source for solving problems over time. Uncover your own assumptions, biases, and dispositions as you write in your journal several times each week.

✓ **Inquiry: Teacher Research as a Tool for Solving Classroom Problems and Enhancing Student Learning**

What questions are arising as you begin your first year of teaching? Questions are good! Find a mentor who can be your daily coach throughout the experience.

_____

_____

_____

Review the *Key Questions* in the PLAN section of this chapter. Which questions are still confusing? List them below and set up a time to discuss them with your cooperating teacher, supervisor, college career center, or Practicum Experiences Office.

_____

_____

_____

✓ **Self-Reflection: Analyze Your Teaching Strategies to Enhance Student Learning**

Which reflective tools will you use as a beginning teacher ?_____

Why?_____

What did you learn about yourself as a teacher through this self-reflection process that will carry you into your first year?

_____

_____

_____

✓ **Critique: Feedback from Your Principal/Department Chair and Mentor to Guide Your Planning, Instructional Practice, and Professionalism**

How will you use other people's feedback as you enter the profession to forward your thinking and learning?

_____

_____

_____

_____